2.95

DRAMA
APPRECIATION
FOR A-LEVEL

JOHN CADDEN

17.

Maria

Edward Arnold
A division of Hodder & Stoughton

Don Gressw BALTIMORE   MELBOURNE   AUCKLAND

First published in Great Britain 1988 by Hodder and Stoughton Educational
a division of Hodder and Stoughton Ltd,
Mill Road, Dunton Green, Sevenoaks, Kent

ISBN 0 340 49507 3

Printed in Singapore by Chong Moh Offset Printing Pte Ltd

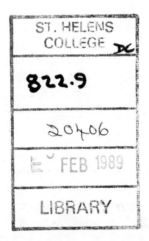
Acknowledgements

We wish to thank the following for permission to reproduce extracts in this book:

Faber and Faber Ltd for an extract from *Waiting for Godot* by Samuel Beckett; **The
Society of Authors on behalf of the Bernard Shaw Estate** for an extract from *Arms and
the Man* by Bernard Shaw; **Penguin Books Ltd** for an extract of *Ibsen: Hedda Gabler and
Other Plays* translated by Una Ellis-Fermor, 1950.

Every effort has been made to contact the copyright holders of extracts reproduced. To
those we have been unable to reach, we offer our sincere apologies and hope they will
take our liberty in good faith.

PREFACE

This book completes a trilogy of titles (*Poetry Appreciation For A-Level, and Prose Appreciation For A-Level*) designed specifically for students preparing for the Advanced Level English Literature examinations. However, as the present book assumes no previous, detailed knowledge of the subject on the part of the reader and as it attempts to cover a wide spectrum of the nature, development and elements of Drama, it will hopefully prove of interest to anyone who enjoys the experience of theatre.

The aims and intentions here are, broadly stated: to foster an interest in, and appreciation of, the work of leading dramatists; to enrich and deepen the understanding and sensitivity of that appreciation by examining the different elements that constitute Drama; to broaden the student's awareness of the development and traditions of Drama, from earliest times to the present day; to guide the student as to how such material should be developed and utilised when approaching Drama for examination purposes; and, finally, to prepare the student for actually tackling examination questions and written assignments in general.

The A-Level student will find this book has a wider scope of reference and relevance than its two predecessors. All examining boards have several dramatists on every year's syllabus and students are unlikely to find themselves concerned exclusively with novelists and poets. Some boards include extracts from plays for critical comment and appreciation, together with the more traditional poetry and prose passages. Finally, and most obviously, it would be difficult to imagine an A-Level English Literature course that did not lead to a sustained and detailed confrontation with the most celebrated dramatist England has produced. With this in mind, an entire chapter is devoted to Shakespeare.

This book, then, has something of a multi-purpose framework and does not seek, specifically, to prepare the student for any *one* single type of examination. This will be in evidence in the exercises, which attempt to offer as much combined and varied practice as possible, bearing in mind the varying skills required in the various A-Level English Literature examinations.

CONTENTS

CHAPTER 1

THE NATURE OF DRAMA

GENERAL CONSIDERATIONS

It is necessary, from the outset, to have a clear idea of what we actually mean by Drama. How can things as diverse as Mime, Restoration Comedy, Victorian Melodrama, the Theatre of the Absurd, Japanese Noh, *Oedipus Rex*, *West Side Story* and *Look Back in Anger* all possibly come under the one "umbrella" of Drama?

The answer lies in the fact that Drama, more than any other literary form, depends upon certain *conventions*. These conventions— or distinct rules of structure, format and presentation—are themselves still open to different interpretations. Many argue, for instance, that Drama, by its very nature, is *not* Literature in the first place. Literature, by definition, depends upon the *written* word. Drama focuses itself upon the *spoken* word—as well as a host of other non-literary things, such as gesture, movement and production (i.e. costume, set, lighting, the director's interpretation, etc.).

There is a further argument that the entire process of Drama— where actors pretend to be real people and the audience pretends to believe that the actors *are* real people—is far too artificial and contrived to be meaningful. A counter-argument maintains the opposite. Once the audience accepts that what they are seeing on the stage is a real representation of human life—what Coleridge called the audience's necessary, but "willing suspension of disbelief"—then Drama, with its living and breathing, moving, three-dimensional creations, becomes the *most* natural and realistic of all the Arts.

We will need to look at these conventions of Drama in detail. They are an integral and unifying part of the medium as a whole and without an awareness of their implications, a true perception of the potential of Drama is impossible.

WHAT IS DRAMA?

To return to the problem of defining Drama, we may broadly state: *Drama is something conceived specifically for performance in a theatre (or equivalent) in front of an audience.* This is by no means as facile or self-evident as it may appear. It is a statement with important implications—implications that lead us to the very heart of what Drama is.

Firstly, our definition reminds us that Drama can only be *fully* appreciated *in performance on the stage.* This, in turn, suggests the importance of the actual stage itself, with its potential for movement, gesture, costume, lighting, scenery and props. The actual script is obviously at the centre of the dramatic process, yet in many ways it is only a "skeleton", or "blueprint", waiting for the actors, director, and set, costume and lighting designers to bring it to life with their own creativity. In this sense, Drama is always much more than the printed words of the text.

Secondly, it highlights the fact that Drama is more "public" and open than other forms of literary communication. (For our present purposes, we may accept that Drama *is* literary; the concept of Drama as a whole may well involve many crucial, non-literary elements, as we have seen above, yet each individual play may be considered in terms of the *written* script which is its very core.) We share the performance with the other members of the audience—and this sense of the "shared experience" is an important aspect of Drama's appeal. Watching a play may well lack the intimacy of sitting alone in deep, quiet contemplation of a novel or poem, yet it frequently provides the memorable experience of joining hundreds of people joying in the antics of a Falstaff, or leaving a theatre in communal, chastened silence after the trials of King Lear.

There are other important implications behind our working definition of Drama. It helps focus our attention on the importance of the audience itself. The subtle, yet symbiotic, psychological relationship between the actual performance and a living, breathing audience constantly affects the way a dramatist writes. The dramatist is also aware of the audience's expectations—and may choose to offer exactly what the audience expects (as in Kyd's *The Spanish Tragedy*), or to offer what the audience expects with certain modifications and innovations (as in Shakespeare's Revenge Tragedies), or to try and change such expectations by offering something completely unfamiliar (as with Shaw, Brecht, the Theatre of the Absurd, or *The Playboy of the Western World*, which actually prompted a riot on its first performance).

This issue of the role of the audience leads to another consideration—one that is somewhat mundane and practical, yet still an important factor. For the poet or novelist, no matter how unappreciated or unread he may be in his own time, a sympathetic publisher will at least guarantee the continuing survival of his work. This may be of little comfort to his bank manager (or his hungry stomach), but it at least means that the determined and dedicated writer can write exclusively *for himself* (in the deepest sense of this phrase). But if the work of the playwright is to survive, then, quite simply, it *must* be performed. Although the playwright will obviously write of issues close to his own heart, he must also write *for an audience*. He must, in some sense of the word, "appeal"—and do so to a sufficient number of his contemporaries. Dr. Johnson speaks for all dramatists when he states:

> The drama's laws, the drama's patrons give,
> For we that live to please, must please to live.

We will see later how this subtle influence of pleasing the patrons can affect the ways in which the dramatist approaches his craft. Yet while the novelist or poet may sit in splendid isolation, ignoring current tastes or trends in his art, dedicating himself solely to what *he* sees as the purity of his own vision and scorning the ignorance of his age for not perceiving his value, the playwright can afford no such luxury. This need to "sell seats" and pander to popular expectations may seem to cheapen the dramatist's art. However, only the second-rate playwright will do this exclusively and it is a salutary thought that no writer for the theatre was ever more aware of the pressing need to fill that theatre than Shakespeare himself.

IMPLICATIONS FOR THE STUDENT

From the above, it may now seem that it is impossible to study Drama other than as it exists in performance. Certainly, at least one viewing of a good performance would be a prerequisite for any ideal course of study on any given play. However, nearly all the student's attention, throughout such a course, will focus on the written text. What is required—and this cannot be emphasised too much—is active, responsive and imaginative reading of the play, on the part of the student, to make that play "come alive". Such reading will carry the student deep into the whole process of Drama. The reader's imagination "sees" and "hears" the play in the theatre of his or her own mind. The reader becomes, in effect, the director—challenged by the script before him to create a "living" performance of the work. In the previous books on poetry and prose, I stressed this basic need for active and creative reading—a need that is far greater, indeed crucial, when we read a play. Shaw once said: "If my readers do their fair share of the work, I daresay they will understand nearly as much of my plays as I do myself." Although Shaw is being somewhat whimsical here, the observation is seriously valid. It is interesting to note that Shaw specifically indicates the *reader* of a play, as opposed to an audience—and of all dramatists, Shaw, with his elaborate and essential Prefaces, character notes and stage directions, intended his work to be read as well as performed.

If the student can develop this facility to create the play in performance in his or her imagination, can learn, in Shaw's words, to do "their fair share of the work", then the problem of seeing the right play, in *actual* performance, at the right time, is largely overcome. It is a vital ingredient in the study of any given play—and even more so when the student approaches "unseen" dramatic extracts for critical comment and appreciation.

EXERCISES

1. Would you prefer to read a novel or see a play? Give full reasons for your choice and consider the different type of "communication" the two experiences offer.
2. Discuss a dramatisation—whether play, film, or television—of a novel you have read. What were the strengths and weaknesses of the dramatisation? How would *your* dramatisation have differed from the one you saw?
3. What do you feel are the main advantages to be gained from (a)

seeing a play in performance, and (b) reading a play on your own?

4. Which is the more effective way of approaching a play—to see it first, in performance, and then read and study it, or to read and study the play first and then see it? Give full reasons for your opinion.

CHAPTER 2

THE ESSENCE OF DRAMA

We have seen how our definition of Drama has imparted some shape and unity to our idea of what Drama is in the first place. There remain two central, core concepts—and one important distinction—which require some understanding before we begin looking at the actual details and elements of Drama.

THE SENSE OF CONFLICT

A sense of conflict—between the individual and his ideals or values, the individual and his environment, the individual and spiritual (even supernatural) forces, or between the individual and other individuals—is frequently important in novels and poems. However, in Drama, it is crucial and ever-present.

Normally, a play will be a self-contained, relatively short (compared with, say, the average-length novel) creation. It will lend itself to an impending sense of *crisis* which will gradually lead to a climax of some sort. The crisis itself inevitably centres on an issue of conflict, while the *climax* will be the decisive action that resolves the crisis one way or the other. This is more obviously the case with tragedy, where the climax will usually be the death or despair of the main character, yet it will also hold true for comedy. Here the tone will be lighter and the impending catastrophe less menacing, yet the sense of conflict will still prevail.

Conflict becomes the crucial element for sustaining dramatic tension and audience interest. The playwright cannot resort too frequently to overly "dramatic" or sensational action—that would detract from the impact of the climax itself. Nor can he "over-write" a particularly striking, colourful or amusing character, as this will disturb the balance of the play as a whole. Yet a sustained and interesting sense of conflict will help keep the audience attentive to the play throughout the course of its performance.

The sense of conflict will be exploited by dramatists in different ways. At its most powerfully straightforward, we can see its potential for tragedy in Macbeth deliberating as to whether or not to kill his king, or in Mark Antony's dilemma in the conflict between his "Roman" self as a ruler of the Empire and his "sensual" self as the lover of Cleopatra. The comic potential of conflict is evident in Jack Worthing's struggles to overcome the importance of *not* being "Ernest", or in the demented charade of Volpone maintaining his disguises. A more subtle use of conflict in comedy is found in *Much Ado About Nothing*—where the conflict between what Beatrice and Benedick really are and what they wish to appear is highlighted in their glitteringly witty mind-games. Even *Waiting for Godot*—on the surface, the least "dramatic" of all plays, where literally nothing (or almost nothing) happens—is centred on the subtle tension, the constant conflict, of whether to actually "wait" or not. Yet perhaps the finest single example of a sustained, almost claustrophobic, sense of conflict is found in Hamlet's full five acts of traumatic, psychological vacillations over avenging his murdered father.

THE QUESTION OF REALISM

In our present context, "realism" may be defined as describing a piece of work that faithfully presents human life *as it is actually lived*. In other words, we are treated to the spectacle of ordinary human beings thinking, feeling and doing the sort of things most of us do, and in the sort of situations most of us find ourselves in, every day of our lives. We are offered a "slice of life" which we can instantly recognise, identify with, and believe in.

Yet if we accept, along with Coleridge, that the audience are prepared to "willingly suspend disbelief" in the theatre and pretend that they are watching real, live people on the stage, it appears that many dramatists renege on *their* part of the "bargain of illusion" by asking the audience to accept unlikely, even incredible characters, situations and behaviour. Greek Drama has recited, poetic speech and deals exclusively with myths and legends. Many dramatists, including modern ones, have their characters using language one would never hear on the streets in daily life. Shakespeare makes full use of magic and the supernatural. Beckett has characters living wholly in dustbins, or buried up to their waist (and later neck) in earth. Drama, as we have said, is a "three-dimensional" art form; its creations breathe, talk and move. It purports to offer a powerful representation of human life. Given, then, the sort of liberties dramatists are apt to take in terms of "realism", why does the whole thing not fall apart?

The answer lies in perceiving the distinction between *surface* or *physical* realism—where the characters, their appearance, their words, etc. are all instantly recognisable—and the sort of realism the dramatist is aiming for. This is more a form of *psychological* realism. For it is the thoughts, the emotions, the desires, the needs, the fears—the *inner life* of human beings—that the dramatist wants to be realistic and ring true in his play.

Once we realise this, we find that surface realism becomes a matter of choice—in terms of technique—on the part of the playwright. He may well choose to have everyday characters caught up in the routine of daily living and exchanging colloquial dialogue—as is the case with *Look Back in Anger*. Such drama is sometimes referred to as "kitchen sink drama" because of its constant (some would say excessive) faithfulness to the seemingly ordinary and mundane. Or the playwright may choose to use kings, emperors, even gods, entangled in fantastic webs of fate and intrigue (which the audience themselves are most unlikely to have encountered)—as in *King Lear*.

Both types of play will have their different appeal. The "slice of life" drama (sometimes called naturalistic) gratifies us by showing the emotion, conflict, tragedy, comedy—"drama", if you like—to be found in everyday life. By subtle implication, our own lives may appear more dramatic, more glamorous and more interesting. On the other hand, we may be captivated by the sort of world and life we can never know, observing the dilemmas before us from a safe, yet enthralling, distance. Yet in the end, both types of play are aiming at the same thing: to use character, dialogue, situation and reaction to show how human beings might think, feel and act in the imagined context. In other words, both aim to achieve *psychological realism*.

8

DRAMA AND THEATRE

One final distinction remains to be drawn. In recent years, Drama has developed as a discipline in its own right and such courses examine, in considerable detail, the actual *mechanics* of Drama. They involve their students in aspects of *theatrecraft* (directing, producing, set design, lighting, costume, make-up, etc.) and *stagecraft* (acting, improvisation, mime, etc.)—and they do this in terms of theory *and* practice. The student is involved in the full "process" of Drama.

The Drama content of an Advanced Level English Literature course is primarily concerned with the *literary* element. It will keep the question of performance and the playwright's use of dramatic technicalities—the *theatre* element—constantly in mind, but its main concern will be the written text in its pure, abstract (i.e. non-performed) form. Interesting and important discussion may well arise as to the type of set design most suited to a particular "set" play, or about ideas concerning the lighting of a certain scene, or the difficulties an actor would encounter in delivering his lines; yet the main core of interest and attention will lie in the play's characterisation, plot, use of language, theme, atmosphere and so on; in other words, the *literary* aspects the play will share with poetry and novels, rather than the *mechanics* of the play in performance; with Drama as Literature, rather than Drama as Theatre.

The following chapters will, in part, attempt some sort of bridge between the two. Although the needs of the Advanced Level Literature student are the primary concern, it is hoped that while such a student is developing the facility for appreciating Drama as Literature, we may also look at certain elements of Drama as Theatre to broaden and deepen the student's perception of Drama as a whole. Again, hopefully, this enriched perception may then be brought to bear in Advanced Level assignments and examinations.

EXERCISES

1. Consider how a "sense of conflict" is used to sustain interest in a play you have recently seen or read, or a film you found particularly memorable.

2. What do you understand by the term "escapist"? What are the attractions of escapist books, plays and films?
3. Do you prefer plays, books and films that are "true to life" and "realistic" or those which offer unusual characters and situations? Give reasons for your preference.

CHAPTER 3

THE FORMS OF DRAMA

Although we must always be careful in the way we use any convenient, neat and tidy "labels" in the study of Literature (Romantic, Classical, Victorian, etc.) and realise that such terms have only a limited, somewhat simplistic, value, we may still usefully categorise certain forms of Drama that have evolved over the centuries. As with life itself, a play will contain many elements and aspects; it is unlikely to be *exclusively* tragic or comic throughout. Yet every play will have a *predominant* sort of mood, tone, thought, feeling and structure which should enable us to define it in terms of the dramatic contexts that follow.

TRAGEDY

Earliest Western Drama concerned itself wholly with the darker, tragic side of human life. As Drama developed, this emphasis on tragedy remained the most significant. Edgar Allan Poe even goes so far as to reverse the idea and see life itself as one long tragic play:

> That the play is the tragedy "Man",
> And its hero the conquering worm.

11

Strangely enough, the word "tragedy" comes to us from the Greek for "a goat-song"; original Greek Drama, which was all tragedy, was recited, or sung, by actors wearing goat-skins. For our present purpose, *"tragedy" refers to a play of a serious nature, dealing with sorrowful or terrible events which lead to a fatal or disastrous conclusion.* Such a play may well include moments of light, even comic, relief, yet the *predominant* tone will be one of *seriousness*. There will be serious themes and issues—such as the meaning of life, Man's relationship (or lack of relationship) with the Divine, questions and issues about morality, politics, or philosophy. There will be serious characters—frequently of high social standing and basically admirable natures—using "serious" language which is likely to be formal, perhaps even elevated and poetic.

Aristotle, the Greek philosopher whose *Poetics* offer many perceptive insights into the whole process of Literature, felt that the aim of tragedy was to arouse "pity and fear" in the audience. We feel *pity* as we sympathise with the plight of fellow human beings suffering great misery, and *fear* because we are reminded of our own vulnerability to Fate, the schemings of others and our own basic character weaknesses (especially, for the Greeks, pride, or *hubris*—where a man forgets he is a man and thinks he is a god). Aristotle also prescribed a basic format for tragedy: it should concern a man of high rank and esteem who has a basically noble character (i.e. one which the audience will, in some way, admire), who is brought to destruction either by a fundamental human weakness (the so-called *fatal flaw*), or by the machinations of others (or Fate)—or by a combination of the two.

If this format appears somewhat restrictive and stereotyped, we need only look to Shakespeare to see its potential for producing tragedies of the highest order. Hamlet, a prince of attractive, even poetic, qualities, is undone (even though his cause is just) by a certain lack of conviction and decisiveness. Romeo, born into the finest of Veronese families, and another youth of compelling charm, is brought low partly through his own character (rash impetuosity), partly through the actions of others (Tybalt's vindictiveness) and partly by Fate (the missed letter from Verona and the mistiming of events in the crypt). Othello is a general of the highest renown, a man of proven worth, dignity and honour, yet he is destroyed by his irrational jealousy, the scheming of Iago and the intervention of Fate on Iago's behalf (the "lost" handkerchief). Macbeth is another general of distinguished service, a man with the respect and trust of his king, yet one who falls victim to over-ambition, the influence of his wife and evil promptings of the supernatural.

Such a list, though admittedly simplified, could easily go on. In other places, Shakespeare seems to toy with the potential for tragedy—the jealousy of Leontes, the lust of Angelo, the desire for revenge in Prospero—before retreating to the safe confines of a "happy" ending.

More modern tragedy, by and large, no longer has the "elevated" or *heroic* element inherent in Aristotle's format, yet the desire to arouse "pity and fear" remains much the same. Aristotle also spoke of another central aspect of the process of tragedy—*catharsis*. This relates to the cleansing or purging effect of tragedy and it applies to both the play and the audience. The tragedy, or the evil that caused it, is "purged" from the final action. Most of Shakespeare's tragedies end with a strong sense of new, optimistic beginnings and a feeling of restored order after chaos—no matter how dire the previous events may have been. Similarly an audience that has viewed and perhaps shared the terrors and misery of the tragic climax, experiences a peaceful serenity at having seen human life pass through and out of the darker side of the human condition.

COMEDY

As soon as we realise this word comes from the Greek for revelry, feasting and celebration, we are immediately aware of the fundamental difference between comedy and tragedy. In this book, the word *"comedy" is used to refer to plays of a light, possibly amusing nature, that end "happily"*. It tends to deal with eccentric or extreme characters and behaviour. Life itself is presented as a comic spectacle, rather than its more serious and disturbing counterpart in tragedy. The style will be "familiar"—i.e. less elevated or poetic than that of tragedy—and frequently humorous. The central characters will engage the audience's sympathy, even affection, and they will not be too seriously threatened by potential disaster—though such a feeling may be present to add pace and tension to the action. The basic aim of comedy, quite simply, is to amuse and please—hence its origins at festivals and celebrations. Nobody wants to think or "feel" too hard when they are out to enjoy themselves.

Just as tragedy may have moments of light relief, comedy may involve itself in more serious issues—especially concerning social behaviour. (As a very broad distinction, tragedy tends to look at Man as a *Universal* creature, while comedy looks at Man as a *Social* animal.)

In its pure sense, comedy need not necessarily strive to be humorous. Yet as it so frequently deals with highlighting (and perhaps ridiculing) the eccentric and the extreme, and does so with a light tone and less profoundly developed characterisation, humorous incidents, characters and language are usually widely in evidence. Through this association, comedy acquired its modern meaning of something actually intended to make us laugh.

Comedy initially aimed to please its audience in a different sense however. It tried to show that behaviour beyond the prescribed social norm was unacceptable and, in the end, unprofitable. The moral transgressions found in comedy were usually the "lower" sins—greed, self-deception, hypocrisy, etc.—rather than the "cardinal" sins of tragedy—pride, murder, lust for power, dishonour, etc. The "villains" of comedy are less threatening than those of tragedy—more wicked than actually evil—and in the end, somewhat petty and abject. They have none of the brooding malevolence of an .Iago or the frightening lack of moral restraint of an Edmund.

Once the main action of comedy was concluded, the dramatist usually sought to leave his audience with an abiding impression of peace, joy and harmony. This led to the tradition of ending comedies with a marriage—a striking image of optimism, togetherness, new beginnings and social order—as the archetypal "happy ending".

Tragedy was born in sombre religious rituals. Comedy's roots (as a diversion or entertainment at festivals) are comparatively humble, yet it has evolved as a complex and subtle form of Drama. Dramatists soon exploited the potential for mixing elements of tragedy and comedy within the one play—and in almost equal measure, rather than as occasional relief from a predominantly serious or light-hearted mood. Such plays are sometimes known as *tragi-comedies*. Their effect on an audience can be deliberately disconcerting—we are never quite sure if it is safe, or right, or "proper" to be amused by what we are seeing. *Waiting for Godot* is a fine example of tragi-comedy in modern times. Shakespeare's *All's Well That Ends Well*, *Troilus and Cressida* and *Measure for Measure*—the so-called "problem plays"—have long confused critics and audiences as to how they should be classified. Technically, they follow the pattern of comedy, yet they create a dark and sombre atmosphere and provide few humorous or "comedic" interludes. In recent times, an even more sinister note has been introduced to create the "black comedy" of a playwright such as Joe Orton.

As we shall see later, comedy has enjoyed a varied development—with such peaks of achievement as Ben Jonson's "comedy of humours", the Restoration "comedies of manners" and the sharp elegance of Oscar Wilde. Two types of comedy have, however, become forms of Drama in their own right; these are *farce* and *satire*.

FARCE

This originally meant "stuffing" and farce was initially a series of jests "stuffed" into comedy for humorous effect. The sole purpose of farce is to excite laughter. As such, its characters, actions and behaviour are even more exaggerated and ridiculous than would normally be found in comedy. The most contrived and fantastic comic dilemmas are devised to create humour. This humour will usually be visual (the classic "trousers falling down" situation) and extremely broad (i.e. unsubtle and undemanding).

Just as the action of the plot is fashioned purely for humorous effect, so too are the undeveloped, often "one-dimensional" characters. Farce is a popular, yet somewhat ephemeral form of Drama; the pleasure derived from it tends to evaporate once the actual performance is over. Only the French, most notably Molière and Feydeau, have created a more enduring and satisfying form of Drama from farce. However, dramatists as varied as Aristophanes, Shakespeare and Stoppard have all made telling use of an element of farce in their plays.

SATIRE

In a sense, this is the most "serious" form of comedy. A satirical play aims to please and amuse—but also to instruct. The satirist wants us to laugh *and* think—appropriately enough when we consider the word initially meant "a mixed dish". As in comedy, the audience is shown extreme forms of character and behaviour, yet these are so ridiculed in satire with the intention of preventing *us* from ever thinking, feeling, or acting in the same way. We are subtly warned that if we should do so, we ourselves would appear as ridiculous and laughable as the characters we see on the stage. In other words, satire involves moral (or perhaps political, or social) criticism.

No matter how humorous or light-hearted the play may appear, the satirical dramatist is usually deeply serious and concerned about the issues he chooses to ridicule, parody, lampoon, or simply be sarcastic about. Perhaps the finest examples we have are Ben Jonson's *The Alchemist* and *Volpone*. Neither before or since have greed and materialism been so ruthlessly, or hilariously, exposed in English Drama.

We have looked at the two major forms of Drama—tragedy and comedy. There are several other forms with which the student should be familiar.

MELODRAMA

This was originally a form of Drama with background musical accompaniment. Melodrama makes violent and unsubtle demands upon the audience's emotions—invariably involving desperate dilemmas or perils (moral or physical, frequently both) for the main character (usually female). The characters tend to be somewhat stereotyped and "one-dimensional", while the action of the plot generally has elements of sensationalism (i.e. contrived and extreme situations designed to terrify or thrill the audience in the most overt manner).

Melodrama was mainly in vogue in Victorian times. It has hardly survived the passage of time, other than as a curious, "period-piece" insight into Victorian tastes. The adjective *melodramatic*, however, is a most useful addition to the student's "dramatic" vocabulary. Many scenes in many plays may be described as "melodramatic"—and often unintentionally so. This would also include Shakespeare—and perhaps even at the height of his dramatic powers; many have argued that the blinding of Gloster in *King Lear* has a strong melodramatic feeling about it.

HISTORICAL DRAMA

Such plays deal with people and events from recorded history. The dramatist may choose to remain as faithful as possible to "known" history—as in Brecht's *Galileo*, or Osborne's *Luther*—or offer his own version of history, as Shakespeare frequently does. Historical Drama will usually be concerned with important and influential figures in the midst of significant, perhaps momentous, events. Because of this, such plays will tend to approach the "seriousness" of tragedy. Indeed, many historical plays—such as Marlowe's *Tamburlaine* and Shakespeare's *Macbeth*—follow the patterns and achieve the effect of "pure" tragedy.

However, the separate categorisation is useful for the student of Drama. The historical dramatist is committed to certain biographical details; he must, at least in part, be true to historical facts as they stand. It deals with "actual" life, rather than "fictional" life, and actual life is rarely all in one shade, or one tone (i.e. neither wholly tragic, nor wholly comic).

The distinguishing classification of Historical Drama offers important implications in the way we may *approach* a play—particularly in the case of Shakespeare. *Julius Caesar*, for instance, is traditionally classed as a tragedy. Seen *as* a tragedy, the play can appear somewhat unsatisfactory. The main character, in terms of tragedy, disappears from the action as early as the first scene of Act Three (although the sense of Caesar's presence dominates the play throughout). This is hardly the normal pattern of tragedy—either in general terms, or even in the Shakespearean context. Some have argued that the play is really the tragedy of Brutus—yet the play's very title would indicate otherwise; Shakespeare invariably follows the tradition of naming his tragedies after the tragic protagonist. Yet if the play is viewed as Historical Drama, then it becomes a rich and complex presentation of the characters and events at the centre of a crucial period in Rome's development. A similar case may also be made for *Antony and Cleopatra* and *Coriolanus*—and it seems to me that a new classification here of Roman Plays, or Roman Histories, would considerably sharpen our critical appreciation of Shakespeare's work as a whole.

Historical Drama, then, may simply be *interesting* throughout, without particularly arousing "fear and pity" or making us laugh (though it may, at times, do both). A play like *Henry V* is neither tragedy nor comedy, yet its constant and irresistible appeal is a testimony to the potential of a specific form of Drama in its own right.

VERSE DRAMA

As the name clearly implies, this relates to plays written in verse. This obviously leads to a very "formal" type of Drama—and, on the surface, the least "realistic", as nobody actually speaks in verse in everyday life. With its obvious emphasis on *language*, it may also be seen as the most literary form of Drama. Some feel that Verse Drama is too contrived, restrictive and unnatural to be "real" Drama—that it is nothing more than poetry delivered while walking about. Yet in the hands of a Milton or Dryden, it can still prove a powerful "dramatic" experience. Its formality and elaborate structure make Verse Drama more suited to serious, elevated and "heroic" characters and issues.

It is important to reserve the title of Verse Drama for plays in which the verse element deliberately calls attention to itself—usually by using rhyme. The plays of Marlowe, Jonson and Shakespeare, for instance, are all technically Verse Drama. They tend to share the slower pace and "heroic" aspects of all Verse Drama, yet they are more properly seen as tragedy or comedy. The unrhymed Verse Drama of the great Elizabethan dramatists was more a matter of tradition and contemporary expectations than a deliberate *stylistic* choice (as is the case with T.S. Eliot, for instance). In normal rhymed Verse Drama, the eloquence and power of expression predominates; in the work of the Elizabethans, it is used more as a positive means of establishing other things—character, atmosphere and situation. Verse Drama obviously also does this, yet we will leave the theatre with the actual *poetry* ringing in our ears. We leave a Shakespearean, Jonsonian, or Marlovian play with a greater sense of having experienced the *total* dramatic process.

MASQUE

Not surprisingly, this was originally used to signify a "masked" entertainment. In Greek Drama, all the actors wore masks, yet *masque* itself as a form of Drama only developed in the seventeenth-century courts of Europe. In these lavish and sumptuous settings, masque concerned itself more with spectacle than plot or character. Drama had finally moved "indoors" and for the first time costume, scenery, lighting and even "special effects" (often involving complex mechanical devices) came into prominence. Masque tended to be somewhat excessive in its use of these new "dramatic toys"—so much so that they were inclined to obscure all other elements of the dramatic experience. Language—always in verse—and character were similarly ornate and stately and the end-product is a somewhat static and non-dynamic series of visual and aural images. These would frequently be enhanced by music and elaborate, stylised mime. The actors were often amateurs—members of the aristocratic elite for whom the plays were almost exclusively designed.

In terms of English Drama, only the masques of Jonson and Milton—which deal with serious moral issues, show some awareness of character development, provide taut structuring and deliver verse of resonant power as well as lyrical eloquence—transcend the limited scope of this form of Drama. It is, however, important for the student of English Literature to understand this concept of Masque Drama. Many dramatists make effective use of such "masque" elements in other, more significant, forms of Drama—most notably mime, dumb-show (where the actors communicate by gesture and movement, rather than speech) and music.[1] It is impossible to appreciate fully Shakespeare's final plays, particularly *The Winter's Tale* and *The Tempest*, without some understanding of the masque tradition. Indeed, mime and music are used extensively throughout Shakespeare and not only in the lighter world of the comedies, where we might reasonably expect to find them. They also occur to great and unexpected effect in plays such as *Hamlet* (the dumb-show re-enactment of the king's murder) and *Antony and Cleopatra* (the haunting music, "under the ground", as Antony's "guardian spirit", Hercules, leaves him).

THEATRE OF THE ABSURD

The final form of Drama to be looked at in this brief survey is a curiously and typically modern development. "Absurd" means literally *out of harmony* and after the inhumane, incomprehensible horror of two immensely destructive world wars, "out of harmony" was exactly what many leading artists and philosophers of the time felt. It seemed that all the beliefs in the progress of civilisation, in the increasing benefits of culture and education and—most frighteningly—in a benign and caring God, had all been an illusion. Man, it seemed, was still as barbaric and uncivilised as he had been in primitive times (perhaps even more so) if he could still impose mass slaughter, concentration camps, extermination programmes and atom

---

[1] Musical Drama—as distinct from Opera—is a form of Drama in its own right. However, it does not usually enter the province of the student of English Literature, although several dramatists, such as Brecht and Stoppard, have experimented most interestingly with the form.

bombs upon his fellow Man. As the numb survivors looked around, they saw Man as a desperate creature "out of harmony" with himself, his fellow Man, his world and his God.

In Drama, such feelings surface in the Theatre of the Absurd. In these plays, traditional values are shown as no longer fulfilling Man's emotional and spiritual needs. Human life is seen as chaotic and aimless, with the individual a helpless victim of technology, bureaucracy and materialism. In *Waiting for Godot*, two tramps become symbols of all mankind. They are dressed in rags, have no proper food, suffer debilitating and embarrassing ailments and spend the entire play idly trying to pass the time. Their moods alternate between excited optimism and quiet despair, as they await the promised arrival of Godot. The name has obvious religious implications (in spite of the author's own denial of this), yet Godot—the one who will put everything right—never comes. The only arrivals to break the monotony are Pozzo—a vicious, blind tyrant—and Lucky, his helpless, mute slave-victim. In the absence of a "Godot", the only path to survival would appear to be to join the oppressor or the oppressed; at least this provides some form of recognisable identity—something the two tramps agonisingly lack.

To emphasise this somewhat frightening view of Man's "lost" position in the scheme of things, Absurd dramatists frequently employ fantastic, or surreal elements. *Rhinoceros*, by Ionésco, actually has human beings change into the great, stomping, horned creatures in the course of the play. Beckett's ironically titled *Happy Days* has the main character buried up to her waist in a mound of earth in the first act and up to her neck in the second—with obvious implications for the third act, had there been one.

Absurd Drama developed mainly in France. Other than in translation, the student of English Literature is only likely to come across the work of Samuel Beckett and Edward Albee. It is too soon to say how future generations will regard the Theatre of the Absurd, which has declined somewhat since its heyday in the fifties (although contemporary dramatists such as Stoppard and Orton still make use of Absurdist elements). Certainly the finest examples of Absurd Drama are likely to stand the test of time as powerful dramatic experiences.

CONCLUSION

The above outline is intended only as a broad background against which individual plays may be viewed. Many plays refuse to conform to convenient labels. They will combine different elements of Drama throughout the course of their performance. *King Lear*, for instance, is commonly held to be a tragedy—and one of the finest ever written. Yet a case can be made for this play exhibiting traces of virtually *all* the forms of Drama listed above. Certainly the dominant mood is one of impending and profound tragedy and the issues involved all have the necessary "high seriousness". Yet there are strong moments of comedy—no matter how dark and desperate that comedy may be. In the strictest sense, the play is Verse Drama and, dealing with the life of an ancient British king, Historical Drama. We have already seen how the blinding of Gloster may be seen as Melodrama, while the old man's imagined leaping from the cliff could almost be seen as "black" Farce. We may even see an Absurdist element in Lear's constant railing against life for being so meaningless and the Fool's strange, yet telling observations, while the bleak, austere set designs commonly employed for this play suggest nothing more than the bare, "elemental" sets used for a play such as *Waiting for Godot*. This phenomenon is in no way unique to *King Lear; Pericles* draws heavily upon tragedy, comedy, melodrama, verse drama, historical drama, masque, mime and music.

One final point remains to be made. The above survey is not in the least exhaustive. It deals with the forms of Drama the student is most likely to encounter. Other forms—such as Kabuki, Noh, Wayang, Musical Drama, etc.—are beyond the scope of this book, being mainly of interest to the specialist student of Drama itself.

EXERCISES

1. Consider one of the plays you are studying. What "form" of Drama do you consider this play to be? Give reasons for your opinion and consider whether or not it employs any other "forms" of Drama.
2. What particular advantages and disadvantages confront the Historical Dramatist?
3. What do you understand by the term "tragi-comic"? Discuss a play, novel, or film that you consider to be tragic-comic.

CHAPTER 4

P L O T

Having looked in general terms at the nature of Drama and the major forms it may take, we can now turn to the specific *elements* of Drama— the constituent parts that make the whole thing actually work on the stage.

We have already mentioned Aristotle's *Poetics*. In this work, he also outlines the six components of Drama as: plot, character, thought, diction, spectacle and music. Even allowing for the complexity and sophistication with which Drama has developed since the sort of plays Aristotle was considering, we may still use his framework, in modified form, as our starting-point.

WHAT IS PLOT?

This word probably derives from the Old French for *conspiracy*. In Drama, it relates to the way the dramatist "conspires"—or, in the modern sense of the word, "maps out"—the arrangement of material his play will use. At a simple level, the plot concerns the *story* of the play—the sequence of events, the twists and turns and complications of what is to happen and the most effective parts of the play in which they are to be placed.

This all requires careful planning if audience attention and interest are to be sustained throughout the play. Ideally, the desired pattern of plot is one which immediately engages the audience's interest and curiosity as to the characters and their situation and then deepens this interest through a series of well-spaced "dramatic" moments, and perhaps unexpected complications, until the audience is totally intrigued and captivated—and eagerly anticipating the play's climax and resolution.

Yet plot is much more than just "story-line". It concerns the entire structure of the play—a structure which should move forward as a unified, dynamic whole. A sense of ordered structure is crucial to effective Drama, even when the actual play itself is about some form of chaos—whether spiritual, social, moral or political.

The Greeks took this need for structure very seriously and actually prescribed rules by which plays had to be written. This is found in the concept of the *Three Unities*—Unity of Time, Unity of Space and Unity of Action. Briefly stated, the "unities" theory maintains that, for a play to have coherence, fluency and positive dramatic movement, it must ensure that:

1. the action of the play covers one continuous period of time—and this should be no longer than the actual time-length of the performance (Unity of Time);
2. the action of the play takes place entirely in one location (Unity of Place);
3. the play has one plot, or "story-line"—and only one (Unity of Action).

Given such specific boundaries, it is easy to see why Greek Drama centres itself around the one crucial action or incident of the myth or legend with which it is dealing. If the play takes place in Thebes, there can be no stage directions such as: "Athens. A day later." Reference is made to events that happen before (and have a bearing on) the main action, yet the play itself, in performance, is concerned exclusively with that one action. Even "action" is perhaps the wrong word. In Greek Drama, this central "action" will inevitably be a dilemma, or a crucial decision and its implications and consequences. All "dramatic" action occurs "off-stage" as it were, and is reported back to the main characters on stage. *Antigone* deals with the ruler Creon's dilemma as to how to treat his niece, Antigone, who has placed personal, family ties before the edicts of the State. The deaths of Antigone's brothers, which prompt the crisis, happen before the

23

play starts, while her own suicide occurs "off-stage" in the course of the play.

As Drama developed, it was only the strictly "Classical" dramatists (like Corneille, in France, and, on occasion, Ben Jonson, in England) who still adhered to the Three Unities. Most playwrights found the concept too restrictive. Shakespeare, for instance, flouts the Unities with almost gay abandon—whether it is Time (*Pericles* covers the history of its hero from youth to old age and requires a running commentary from Gower—"Only I carry winged time"—to summarise the "missing" years), Space (*Antony and Cleopatra* ranges freely across the empire—Rome, Alexandria, Athens, Messina, Actium), or Action (virtually all the plays have at least one *sub-plot*—i.e. a secondary storyline that is related to the main plot, yet not, in the narrow sense, necessary to it).

The Unities, however, remain an important dramatic concept. Many practising dramatists have sensed the potential for intensity and impact that using one main story, taking place entirely in one fixed location, within the actual time-span of the performance, can achieve. The action appears entirely plausible—the audience requires little "willing suspension of disbelief" to cover awkward changes of set or shifts in time. There are no diversions of any kind to distract the audience from the central characters—their situation, their actions, their thoughts and feelings. The plot acquires a natural, in-built and taut structuring. It is interesting to note that it is in certain of the more intense tragedies (*Hamlet, Othello, King Lear*) that Shakespeare comes closest to observing (i.e. following) the theory of the Three Unities.

THE TECHNICALITIES OF PLOT

For pragmatic reasons of allowing an audience to follow the action of a play as clearly as possible, most dramatists, whatever form of Drama they may be using, will tend to employ the following pattern in arranging their plot:

1. **exposition** – this opening section of the play will introduce the main characters and the sort of people they are; it will also give their background situation and begin to develop the dramatic relationships between them;

2. **dramatic incitement**   – this will be the action or incident which will prompt, encourage, direct, or make necessary the main action of the play;

3. **complication** – this is usually the largest part of the play and will portray the manner in which the characters react to the dramatic incitement (and any further, unforeseen developments arising from it); the incitement may be a moral dilemma, which the characters now try to resolve, or a potential disaster which they attempt to prevent or escape;

4. **crisis**   – this is the climax of the play—the moment when the full implications and consequences of the dramatic incitement must be faced; at this point of crisis, the main characters will either overcome the challenge, or be defeated by it, or perhaps be left somewhere between the two;

5. **resolution**   – the final section of the play, where the strands may be brought together and the "loose ends" tied; the success, or failure, or at least survival of the main characters will be assessed and implications for the future suggested; in traditional Drama, this is where evil is punished and virtue rewarded.

This patterning will make more sense if we look at it "in action", through a couple of working examples. According to our format, *The Merchant of Venice* would look something like this:

1. **exposition**   – the introduction of all the main characters and such important background information as: Antonio being a rich merchant of considerable generosity to his friends; Bassanio's love for Portia and his need for money; Shylock's self-made wealth as a money-lender, his despised position in Venetian society and the hostility he nurses towards those who see him as less than human;

2. **dramatic incitement**   – Antonio borrows money from Shylock and seals the contract with the strange bond of a "pound of flesh";

3. **complication** – the "loss" of Antonio's ships; Jessica's elopement

with Lorenzo; Shylock's growing passion for revenge; the growing interest in events of Portia;

4. **crisis** – the court scene, with Shylock's insistence on "justice" and the climax of Portia's "eleventh hour" intervention;

5. **resolution** – the punishment of Shylock; the recovery of Antonio's fortune; the happiness of Bassanio and Portia, Jessica and Lorenzo.

With *Macbeth*, we find something like this:

1. **exposition** – Macbeth established as a proven and successful general, much trusted and honoured by his king; the background of blood, war and violence at the time is also revealed;

2. **dramatic incitement** – this falls relatively early in the play (Act I, scene iii) with the "prophecies" and goadings of the witches —although the complete incitement is finalised by Lady Macbeth's influence in convincing Macbeth of the desirability of killing the king, at the very end of the act;

3. **complication** – this begins with the troublesome question of Banquo, then develops with Malcolm seeking to claim his rightful throne with English aid; we also have Banquo's ghost, Lady Macbeth's madness and death, further misleading prophecies from the witches—which encourage a dangerous and irrational over-confidence in Macbeth—and Macduff's great desire for revenge;

4. **crisis** – the attack on Macbeth's castle and the combat with Macduff;

5. **resolution** – the death of Macbeth; the satisfied revenge of Macduff; the restoration of the throne to rightful hands and a new sense of order after the demented chaos of Macbeth's short reign.

EXERCISES

1. Consider two plays with which you are familiar. Summarise all the essential details of the plot, in terms of story-line, using no more than two or three sentences for each.
2. Analyse the plays you are studying in terms of exposition, dramatic incitement, complication, crisis and resolution, as outlined in the above examples.

CHAPTER 5

CHARACTER

To a large extent, all Drama depends upon the playwright achieving a full and engaging sense of "character". Yet the nature of Drama means that the methods of characterisation will be very different from those of the novel. The novelist may delve deep into the mind and heart of his characters and provide the most detailed and intimate insights into what these characters are thinking and feeling. Other than using occasional "asides" and soliloquies, the dramatist cannot do this. How, then, *does* the dramatist attempt to create a "rounded" and satisfying sense of character?

STAGE PRESENCE

The first thing a dramatist can do in terms of establishing a character is to use the *physical presence* on the stage of that character to suggest certain things about the "inner" person. This will obviously relate to the immediate impact of the character's physical appearance, movement about the stage, physical actions, use of gesture, intonation and tone of voice in the delivery of lines and so on. These effects of "stage presence"—and the type of costume, make-up and lighting in which they are presented—will, to a considerable degree, depend on how the director and actor read and interpret the part. This is the "grey area" of Drama, where we cannot always be sure we are seeing the play, in its physical appearance, as the dramatist would have desired. However, if the play is carefully and sensitively considered by its producers, any such interpretations should have been inherently suggested by the text itself.

With this physical element of "stage presence", we tend to make judgments about characters in Drama in much the same way as we do in everyday life. We are struck by first impressions, by the way characters *appear*, by their movements and gestures, by the *way* they speak as much as by what they actually have to say. We may not see the "inner" being—the deeper thoughts, feelings, fears, desires—*directly*, as we do in the novel. Yet we do glimpse subtle hints and delicate insights into that inner being as it is manifested and implied in the appearance, words and deeds the character chooses to reveal to the "outer" world—which is exactly what we do, day in, day out, in the complex inter-relationships of our normal lives.

In this way, a character's stage presence will begin to indicate the inner being before a single word is spoken. This will work for all the main characters—and not just the obvious cases of a Richard III, an Othello, or a Shylock. If the actors and director have translated the stage persona into an accurate and relevant physical "creation", then our first impressions will lead us into insights as to what sort of "people" we have before us.

DEEDS AND WORDS

The most obvious means by which we begin to understand a character's "inner being" will come with what they say and what they do. In a perfect world, the two would always go together—our actions would always be in keeping with our ideals and values. Yet the world of Drama, like the real world, is far from perfect. It is often with the significant disparity between what a character says and what he does that we achieve real insight into the inner being.

When we question why a character expresses certain values yet performs contrary actions we are beginning to look deeply into that character. This dichotomy between deeds and words is central to most Shakespearean characters. The difference between the two may be deliberate, as in the case of Iago and Edmund, where it reveals the extent of their ruthless, Machiavellian opportunism. In another way, the variations between the *public image* and the *inner self* may centre on a genuine crisis concerning the identity of the "real" self—as with the Mark Antony of *Antony and Cleopatra*. It may be forced on the character by external forces—as with Brutus—or simply arise through an accidental quirk of fate, as with Hamlet.

A character's *words* provide the context against which his or her *actions* may be judged. In this way, we will sense a character's nobility, or self-sacrifice, or deviousness, or lack of self-knowledge, or hypocrisy. Ignoble deeds, such as Othello's murder of Desdemona, may be extensively modified by the character's own words concerning such actions. The *truth* concerning the inner being of a dramatic character, in terms of words and deeds, invariably lies somewhere between the two.

SOLILOQUY AND ASIDE

A *soliloquy* is an expanded and developed speech in which a dramatic character speaks his thoughts out loud, for the audience alone. What he says is unheard by the other characters in the play. An *aside* is a similar device—though much shorter, often only a single observation, perhaps even just one word. The soliloquy is delivered by the speaker, alone on an otherwise empty stage. An aside is a "stage whisper" by one character to the audience, while other characters present on stage engage in their own dialogue and movement at the same time.

These devices represent attempts by the dramatist to offer the deeper, inner thoughts of a character. It is obviously a significant aid to the full development of a rounded dramatic character to be able to convey such intimate thoughts and feelings. The privacy of being "unheard" by the play's other characters allows the speaker to reveal his or her *true* self; there is no need to maintain a public image or persona. Indeed, we only fully perceive the characters of such powerful dramatic creations as Faustus, Iago, Lady Macbeth and Edmund from their celebrated soliloquies. In *Hamlet*, the entire progress (or non-progress) of the main character's constant moral and psychological dilemma is charted out most clearly in the series of soliloquies. In fact, in this play, the compelling effect of these soliloquies ("O, that this too, too solid flesh would melt", "O, all you host of heaven", "O, what a rogue and peasant slave am I", "To be, or not to be", "'Tis now the very witching time of night", "Now might I do it pat", "How all occasions do inform against me") has, over the years, tended to overshadow all other aspects of the play.

A character will use a soliloquy when most distressed (as we have just seen above in the number of Hamlet's soliloquies that open with a distraught "O"), confused ("To be, or not to be"), scheming ("Now might I do it pat") or optimistic (as in Iago's almost complacent "And what's he, then, that says I play the villain"). In other words, the soliloquy offers crucial insights into a character at times of greatest stress, tension, concentration, yearning or suffering. The combination in the soliloquy of privacy and crisis will lead the character to reveal the true, inner self.

The short, light, rapier thrust of the aside makes it more suited to comedy than tragedy (although there are many striking asides in tragedy, such as Othello's agonised "O, hardness to dissemble" and Iago's gloating "Work on,/My medicine, work"). Asides may be directed at one of the other characters on the stage, yet still "out of earshot" of the rest, rather than at the audience. A marvellous example of this type of aside is sustained throughout *Volpone*—initially with Mosca's "encouragement" of the "gulls", then later in the glorious "bargaining" in court with his master, Volpone, as he bargains to save the latter from punishment "at a price".

There is, however, a problem with soliloquy and aside. Even allowing for their effectiveness within the context of a particular play, where we accept the device as plausible, it remains a somewhat artificial means of characterisation—a form of "dramatic licence" which can strain the audience's sense of credibility. We may all of us talk to ourselves at times, or toss the occasional aside at a friend or colleague while someone else is speaking, yet we would never do so in the manner of the dramatic soliloquy. It is a device that is only suited to "formalised" Drama and, as such, has been largely abandoned by playwrights as a dramatic device. The Elizabethan age was the last age of the great dramatic soliloquy. Dramatists in more recent times have largely ignored the advantages of using the device for fear its unnaturalness may stretch their audience's "willing suspension of disbelief" a little too far. They have chosen to suggest and imply character, rather than state it directly. This has promoted greater realism in dramatic characterisation, as well as introducing a more subtle sophistication into dramatic portraits.

REPORT

Another means of developing characterisation within the relatively short span of a play's performance is by *report*—i.e. the sort of things the *other* characters have to say about the character in question. This may be used to fill in background biographical details—what the character has said or done in the past, or "off-stage"—or it may be used to express opinions as to the type of person the character under discussion might be—the virtues and weaknesses as perceived by those who "know" the character better than we, the audience.

Yet we must be careful with characterisation by report. We must take into account the character and situation of the *speaker* before accepting what he has to say about others as valid or accurate. The speakers may lack insight into the real, inner self of the character they are contemplating—as is the case with Henry IV and Falstaff concerning Prince Hal. Or the speaker may himself be dishonourable and not committed to the actual truth. He may have a personal, ulterior motive, or a grievance to bear, when criticising a character before others. We weigh all these factors together before making our own judgments about the character "under the microscope".

We can see this clearly in *Othello*. We accept that Iago has a keen insight into human nature—which he uses malevolently to his own purpose. As such, we accept that his observations on Othello's naivety and unthinking magnanimity have some validity—yet we do not accept his version of Othello as a gullible simpleton.We balance Iago's version of Othello against Iago's own jealousy, cynicism, sense of injustice and desire for revenge. We then balance this against our own impression of Othello, recalling the dignified bearing and the noble and honourable values by which he lives. Finally we consider the "report" of other more reliable characters—the love of Desdemona, the esteem and affection of Cassio and the admiration of the Duke of Venice. From this potpourri of characterisation ingredients, we are left to draw our own conclusions as to the "real" Othello.

A fine example of the potential depth and subtlety of characterisation by report comes in *Julius Caesar*. Caesar himself appears for only fleeting moments in the play—and he disappears entirely from the action before we are halfway through. Yet the *sense* of Caesar's character—his strengths and weaknesses—dominate and determine the action throughout. The little we do see of Caesar "in person" is enough to suggest a powerful confidence (perhaps bordering on arrogance and complacency), a strong sense of personal worth and a certain susceptibility to flattery. Yet the huge, haunting shadow of Caesar's character comes to us largely by report. It lies somewhere between the admiring, yet reserved comments of Brutus (shaded by Brutus's "black and white" sense of Republican values), the pointed objections of Cassius (influenced by Cassius's sense of *his* own worth) and the unstinting praise of Mark Antony (which is considerably complicated by Antony's gratitude and love to Caesar and *his* own sense of opportunism and desire for self-advancement).

Types of Character

As we look at the development of Drama's traditions, certain recurring *character types* are clearly identifiable. The most significant of these are listed below:

The protagonist

This is the main character in the play, the person at the heart of the main action, conflict or dilemma. Most plays have one or two protagonists. A play will lose much of its concentrated impact if the audience is required to focus its main attention on too many major characters. Tragedies certainly require only one or two protagonists to sustain their intensity. It is usually in Historical Drama, such as *Henry IV* and *Julius Caesar*, that interest may be successfully spread across several characters. The terms *hero* and *heroine* may also be used for the protagonists—although confusion may arise from the modern connotations of these words as people who are noble and admirable. This is strictly not necessary; Richard III is the "hero" of the play that bears his name—yet hardly a heroic figure in the modern sense.

The confidant

This is the trusted friend or colleague in whom the protagonist will confide his or her innermost thoughts or feelings. As such, the confidant becomes a most useful dramatic device for characterisation in depth—and is a far more satisfactory and natural device for allowing such revelations of the "real" protagonist than the soliloquy. The confidant may be a simple, undeveloped sounding-board whose role is merely to listen—as with Nerissa in *The Merchant of Venice*, or Algernon, in *The Importance of Being Earnest*—or they may be developed as important dramatic characters in their own right, as Enobarbus is in *Antony and Cleopatra*.

The Clown/Fool

This is the character charged with injecting, or sustaining, moments of comic relief. Under the guise of foolish simplicity—often a mask for shrewd insight and even wisdom—and under the protection of the "jester's licence", these figures comment humorously on the main characters and their actions, mocking pretensions and hypocrisy and irritating the "villains". They may be straightforward clown figures or highly developed and central dramatic figures, as with the Fool in *King Lear*. They may not always technically be called "fools" or "clowns". The comic relief in the sombre world of *Hamlet* is provided, in different ways, by Osric and the grave-digger.

Stock characters

Occasionally, a dramatist may resort to obvious, even clichéd and stereotyped stock characters—the jealous husband, the greedy merchant, etc.—to populate his stage. Significant Drama usually avoids such "shallow" creations, although Ben Jonson develops stock characters to a marvellously effective level in his major comedies.

CONCLUSION

The process of dramatic characterisation, then, is a complex one. It involves the appearance, bearing and manner of that character (stage presence), the opinions, beliefs and emotions the character expresses (both in public and private), the actions performed, and also what other characters may have to say about him or her. As the above examples have implied—and as in real life—our ultimate assessment will draw upon all these sources. We will not blindly accept the way characters choose to present themselves to the outside world, as a person's *self*-image is not always the *true* self. Much great Drama is, in any case, about the search for true self-knowledge. We draw our conclusions from all the evidence—and if that evidence has been skilfully presented, our conclusions will probably be the same as the dramatist's and the sort of feelings he wants us to adopt towards his creation.

EXERCISES

1. Consider a play you may have seen, read, or studied recently. Given unlimited financial resources, draw up a cast list for that play using famous actors and actresses from film and television with whom you are familiar, giving full reasons as to why you think they would be suitable.

2. Consider three or four main characters from a play you are studying. Draw up a list of character traits for each one, as revealed in the play. Indicate beside each trait your characterisation source (i.e. stage presence, the things the character says, or does, soliloquy, report, etc.) for making such an observation.

3. Consider the protagonist in the play you are studying and show how the *other* characters in the play are used to reveal the protagonist's "true" nature.

CHAPTER 6

THOUGHT

All literary works are concerned with *thought*—ideas, themes, viewpoints, perhaps even a philosophy of life. The writer has something to convey about the important issues of human life—either directly, in his own voice (as in poetry), or indirectly, through fictional creations (as in the novel and Drama). As such, this element of thought will have a crucial relevance to the work's overall meaning and intended purpose.

Meaning is a thorny issue in literature. Some people concern themselves exclusively with a work's "meaning" and neglect the other elements (plot, character, imagery, etc.). Others see writers as craftsmen who should fashion artistic creations and leave philosophy to the philosophers. Others feel (especially students of Advanced Level English Literature) that there is a tendency to "read too much" into literary works, in a search for "deep" meanings that are not there, or at least were not intended by the author.

Writers themselves tend to be touchy about the meaning of their work. D.H. Lawrence felt that you could not "nail" down the meaning of a novel; if we try to do so, we either "kill the book, or the book gets up and walks off with the nail". When T.S. Eliot was asked for the "message" of *The Waste Land*, he replied, simply: "I am a poet, not a postman. I don't deliver messages." When an actor playing Clov in Beckett's *Endgame* asked the dramatist himself for the meaning of his line: "If I knew the combination to the larder, I would kill you",

Beckett replied: "The line means that if you knew the combination to the larder, you would kill him."

As ever, the truth lies somewhere between all these different viewpoints. Literature, Drama included, does involve, promote and require 'thought'. Yet while this "thought" behind the work may often prove the most provocative or satisfying aspect of the work (as is frequently the case, ironically, with Lawrence, Eliot and Beckett), it remains, ultimately, a work of *art* and not a philosophical treatise. "Thought", therefore, is *one element*—no matter how important or impressive in its own right—to be harmoniously and structurally integrated with all the other elements to provide the *total* experience the work seeks to achieve.

TWO TYPES OF THOUGHT

In terms of Drama, we must distinguish between two types of thought in a play. These are: a) the ideas, opinions, values and beliefs expressed overtly by the actual characters, and b) the themes and beliefs and philosophy the dramatist attempts to make the play as a whole *imply*. The sort of "thought" to be found in b) will invariably represent the *view of the world* and values the playwright himself holds.

We have already seen how Drama frequently centres itself around a sense of conflict. This conflict, especially in "traditional" Drama, often arises from the collision of different beliefs, values and ideologies amongst the main characters. The "thought" behind such conflict may be political (as in *Julius Caesar*), moral (as in the struggle between the half-brothers, Edmund and Edgar, in *King Lear*), or philosophical (as in *Doctor Faustus*). It may be presented with full tragic seriousness (as we find in the "duty" versus "personal fulfilment" conflict in *Antony and Cleopatra*), or with a comic semi-seriousness (as in *Arms and the Man*, which places the abstract notion of military honour against the practical, basic need for survival at all cost).

The "thought" of the characters in such situations will further add to the characterisation—often with interesting complications, as in noble ideals maintained by ignoble characters (most notably Angelo in *Measure for Measure*)—as well as being of interest in its own right. The ideas expressed become even more stimulating for an audience if they are specifically challenged within the play by conflicting values or difficult circumstances (as with Angelo again, falling prey to the lust he so condemns in others). As such, we are interested in creations such as Brutus, Cassius and Mark Antony not only as *characters*, but also as *political theorists*.

It is the second type of dramatic thought—the playwright's own thinking—that will ultimately concern us most. By "reading between the lines", as it were, of the characters, situations, events and language—and the way they are arranged towards the eventual outcome—we will sense the dramatist's own values and beliefs about the world and the sort of people with whom it is inhabited.

There are obvious difficulties here. When the main characters are powerfully and persuasively presented, it may be tempting to equate such dramatic capability for characterisation with authorial support and backing. With basically evil characters, no matter how compellingly created (Iago, Lady Macbeth, Edmund), this will not present a problem. Yet other notable dramatic creations (Richard II, Mark Antony, Coriolanus) are far more equivocal. Clearly their presentations reveal some authorial "sympathy" and the alternative modes of "thinking" presented in the plays (Bolingbroke, Octavius Caesar, Aufidius and the Tribunes) are provided by unattractive, "unsympathetic" characters. Yet the resolution of such plays clearly suggests that the beliefs of the main characters are crucially and centrally flawed.

Such ambiguity or ambivalence concerning the playwright's stance towards his main creations can often be a source of dramatic tension and part of the play's overall strength. Our attitudes to people and the beliefs they hold, in life itself, are seldom a clear-cut matter of "black and white" judgments. Yet even the most skilful dramatist must avoid the temptation of over-elaboration and thereby losing sight of his main intention and objective. Shakespeare is sometimes accused of doing just this with a character such as Falstaff. The argument here states that, in the overall scheme of the Henry IV and V cycle of plays, Falstaff should represent the seductive attraction of selfish, physical indulgence that can beset any ruler. However, his vitality and humour are so pervasive and compelling, that the audience tends to sympathise much more with the warmth of Falstaff's world than the coldness of the king's neurotic world of duty. For this reason, Hal's casting off of Falstaff, which, in terms of Shakespeare's political thinking on the "ideal" king, is essential, genuinely shocks and discomforts the audience with its seemingly unnecessary brutality. The character appears to have "grown out of proportion" and disturbed the balance of "thought" in the play. A similar charge is often laid against Ben Jonson with Volpone. Although this character spends the entire play in a petty charade of avarice and deceit, we are actually drawn to him, rather than repelled by him. This is because he is portrayed with such colour, eloquence and voluptuous grandeur in comparison with the seedy, grubby little parasites that surround him. (Even the figures of "virtue" are deliberately insipid, one-dimensional and unappealing in this play.)

However, in both these instances, we can still perceive the dramatists' "thought" working at a deeper level beneath the surface appearance. We can still enjoy, even admire, the sharp, cynical wit and passionate hedonism of Falstaff, or the charm, style and eloquence of Volpone—especially when we observe their "colleagues" who are, for the most part, mercenary, scheming, unscrupulous, witless, naive, or unthinking—without seeing them as embodiments of the dramatists' own philosophy of life. To do so, we would be completely missing the play's more subtle "thought"—and turning the playwrights' own immense skills of characterisation as evidence against them.

Once the dramatic conflict of the *characters'* beliefs and values has been established, the audience will begin to sense the playwright's own thought unfolding in the struggles between the various extremes. No matter how much we may be swayed by the powerful self-reliance of Edmund, or the sharp intelligence and invention of Iago, at the expense of the simple (and less dramatically impressive) decency and nobility of Edgar and Othello, we invariably come to perceive these characters as the dramatist wishes us to see them. Indeed, if the dramatist wishes us to have any admiration, sympathy and respect for his protagonist, then the workings of evil (and the characters who embody it) *must* be displayed in all their seductive attractiveness. We are otherwise likely to dismiss the protagonist as impressionable, gullible and weak-minded. It is rare for one character to stand *wholly* for the dramatist's own "thought" on the themes at issue in a play. It is possible to see Henry V as some sort of approximation to Shakespeare's thinking on the ideal king and, on occasion, a character may utter much of the dramatist's known philosophy of life (as with Shaw's John Tanner). Usually, however, the dramatist's thought and philosophy of life will be a modification—distillation, perhaps—of the various views expressed in the play and the way those embodying such views are treated in the final resolution.

EXERCISES

1. List all the major characters in the plays you are studying. Outline

briefly the sort of values, beliefs and opinions they would appear to stand for, as revealed in the play. Give evidence for your observations.

2. Using your completed list from the previous question, indicate which of those values, beliefs and opinions the action and outcome of the play as a whole seems to uphold and those which are not endorsed. Again, give full reasons for your opinions.

3. Consider a character in one of the plays you are studying whose beliefs and values are clearly "wrong", perhaps even immoral. By what means does the dramatist manage to make this character interesting and perhaps even admirable in some way to the audience?

4. Consider carefully one of the plays you are studying. What do you feel are the main *themes* and *issues* at the centre of the play? What do you take to be the dramatist's *own* thinking on these issues?

CHAPTER 7

DICTION

We will use diction here to refer to the type of language used in the play. We will not use it specifically for dialogue. Although dialogue uses language in a most obvious way, it is properly viewed as a dramatic technique and element in its own right.

The diction, or type of language (formal, serious, colloquial, slang, etc.) will lend colour, atmosphere and tone to the play as a whole and will also relate to specific characterisation, as the *manner* of expression will further increase our perception of that character as much as what he or she actually says.

DICTION AND MOOD

The language used predominantly in any given play will have a crucial influence on the type of *mood* the play seeks to achieve. If the diction is formal and philosophic, it will help create the sense of seriousness most suited to tragedy. Take, for instance, Faustus's:

> My heart's so harden'd, I cannot repent:
> Scarce can I name salvation, faith, or heaven,
> But fearful echoes thunder in mine ears,

"Faustus, thou art damn'd!" then swords, and knives,
Poison, guns, halters, and envenom'd steel
Are laid before me to despatch myself;
And long ere this I should have slain myself,
Had not sweet pleasure conquer'd deep despair.

This is formal in the sense that it *is* not (nor in Elizabethan terms, *was* not) everyday speech. The diction is "elevated" ("envenom'd", "conquer'd") to suit the serious philosophic issues (salvation, repentance, suicide). Yet there is nothing "dry" or academic about this language. Its dramatic strength lies in the creation of a sombre and intense mood through the poetic resonance of the diction ("fearful echoes thunder in mine ears") to reflect the speaker's agitated and excited unease.

Conversely, the lighter mood and more rapid movement of comedy is frequently best served by the informal, colloquial, even racy, language that we find in *The Way of the World*:

The fashion's a fool; and you're a fop dear
brother. 'Sheart, I've suspected this—by'r
Lady, I conjectured you were a fop since you
began to change the style of your letters, and
write in a scrap of paper gilt round the edges,
no bigger than a subpoena. I might expect this
when you left off "Honoured Brother", and "Hoping
you are in good health", and so forth—to begin
with a "Rat me, knight, I'm so sick of last
night's debauch—'ods heart."

Such a masterful rendition of colloquial diction and inflection ("Sheart", "by'r Lady", "Rat me") and control of the almost breathless rhythmic intonations (where the use of punctuation is most effective) lend great pace and colour to the play as a whole, as well as making the portraits of Sir Wilfull (the speaker) and Witwoud (the subject) extremely vivid.

These are, perhaps, the two most obvious extremes of diction in Drama. There are almost as many varying shades in between as there are individual dramatists. Oscar Wilde develops an elaborate, ornate fluency of language as the medium for the elegant sophistication of his comedies, as in this classic exchange from *The Importance of Being Earnest*:

JACK: My dear Algy, I don't know whether you will be able to
          understand my real motives. You are hardly serious

enough. When one is placed in the position of guardian, one has to adopt a very high moral tone on all subjects. It's one's duty to do so. And as a high moral tone can hardly be said to conduce very much to either one's health or one's happiness, in order to get up to town I have always pretended to have a younger brother of the name of Ernest, who lives in the Albany, and gets into the most dreadful scrapes. That, my dear Algy, is the whole truth pure and simple.

ALGERNON: The truth is rarely pure and never simple. Modern life would be very tedious if it were either, and modern literature a complete impossibility!

Here, the diction flows with a cultured and urbane smoothness, moving through delightful linguistic touches ("can hardly be said to conduce") to the well-prepared, diamond-tipped wit of Algernon's reply.

Yet the refined and elegant language of the nineteenth-century middle-class drawing-room was used very differently by another dramatist. Ibsen uses it to both cover and enhance the psychological tension and turmoil that lies just beneath the surface in such lives, as in *Hedda Gabler*:

BRACK [looking steadily at her]: Ejlert Lövborg meant more to you than you are perhaps willing to admit to yourself. Or am I wrong there?

HEDDA: I don't answer that kind of question. I only know that Ejlert Lövborg had the courage to live life in his own way. And now—this great deed, with all its beauty? That he had the strength and will to break away from the feast of life ... and so early.

BRACK: I am very sorry, Madam Hedda, but I must deprive you of your pretty illusion.

HEDDA: Illusion?

BRACK: Which you would have been deprived of soon, in any case.

HEDDA: And what is it?

BRACK: He did not shoot himself intentionally.

Here, the rather precious and self-conscious delicacy of language (most notably the "turn[ing] away from the banquet of life" euphemism for suicide) and the melodramatic tone of Hedda (captured in the dramatic punctuation of exclamations and dashes) say much about Hedda's character. Yet, in conjunction with Brack's similar turns of expression ("amiable illusion"), the language helps sustain the play's broader atmosphere of a somewhat unreal and vulnerable world, whose inhabitants are not completely in touch with their own inner selves or external reality.

From the self-regarding eloquence of the nineteenth-century drawing-room, we may move to the work of a dramatist who constantly seeks to reduce language to its barest essentials. The language of Beckett's plays is as stark and as elemental as the characters and settings, yet still infused with a strange and haunting poetic quality, as in *Waiting for Godot*:

ESTRAGON: All the dead voices.
VLADIMIR: They make a noise like wings.
ESTRAGON: Like leaves.
VLADIMIR: Like sand.
ESTRAGON: Like leaves.

[Silence]

VLADIMIR: They all speak together.
ESTRAGON: Each one to itself.

[Silence]

VLADIMIR: Rather they whisper.
ESTRAGON: They rustle.
VLADIMIR: They murmur.
ESTRAGON: They rustle.

Twentieth-century studies of Shakespeare have explored the way in which language becomes a central part of the play's purpose. This is most obvious in the plays that employ *thematic imagery*—where a specific type of image and language is used throughout the play (and by various speakers) to establish a persistent mood and direction of thought. Images of rotten decay, expressed in powerfully disconcerting images, constantly thread their way through *Hamlet* to convey the central character's obsession that there really is something "rotten" at the core of life in general and "the state of Denmark" in particular . In *Othello*, the diction is largely rooted in military terms, even the declarations of love ("O my fair warrior" is Othello's greeting to Desdemona after their separation at sea), to suggest the only type of reality and terms of reference that Othello can comprehend. In *King Lear*, the protagonist's growing sense of Man's insignificance in a vast universe is subtly developed in the increasing use of images of the "lowest" creatures—especially insects ("As flies to wanton boys are we to the gods").

DICTION AND CHARACTER

As we have already noted above with *Hedda Gabler*, language is crucial in the development of character. We will form impressions from the type of expression used as much as from what is expressed. In many cases, a character's language will take us to the very heart of the inner personality. Othello is a fine example of this subtle use of characterisation through language. Take, for instance, his speech to the Venetian Senate:

> Most potent, grave, and reverend signiors,
> My very noble and approv'd good masters,—
> That I have ta'en away this old man's daughter,
> It is most true; true, I have married her:
> The very head and front of my offending
> Hath this extent, no more. Rude am I in my speech,
> And little bless'd with the soft phrase of peace;
> For since these arms of mine had seven years' pith,
> Till now some nine moons wasted, they have us'd
> Their dearest action in the tented field;
> And little of this great world can I speak,
> More than pertains to feats of broil and battle;
> And therefore little shall I grace my cause
> In speaking for myself. Yet, by your gracious patience,
> I will a round unvarnish'd tale deliver...

Here, the language speaks volumes of the man's sense of dignity, propriety, honour, justice and responsibility. Yet the language implies something far more subtle and essential about Othello's character. I used the word "speech" and that is exactly what Othello engages in. He does not *talk* to people, he makes speeches *at* them. The language is florid, elaborate and self-conscious (especially in its obvious "poetic" touches—"feats of *b*roil and *b*attle"). The language itself is so formal (as in the grandiloquent opening two-line address) that it makes nonsense of Othello's belief that he is "rude" in speech, as does the elaborate narration that follows the preface of a "round *unvarnish'd* tale". What we have here is a man out of touch with daily reality (he confesses as much himself—"little of this great world can I speak"); a man who has a fixed image of himself that will later be destroyed, leaving him without an identity to live with and by; and a man who has illusions of life reduced to the simple, clear-cut issues of a military engagement.

A final example of how language can be used with such sophistication in characterisation may be found in *Richard II*. The king has just been deposed by Bolingbroke:

> Let's talk of graves, of worms, and epitaphs;
> Make dust our paper, and with rainy eyes
> Write sorrow on the bosom of the earth.
> Let's choose executors, and talk of wills:
> And yet not so,—for what can we bequeath,
> Save our deposed bodies to the ground?

Once again, the words impress superficially. We sense an intelligent sensitivity, a cultured and poetic sensibility and a regal manner. Yet the language itself ("rainy eyes", "our deposed bodies") and its weary rhythms also suggest, at a deeper level, the lackadaisical, indulgent, passive self-pity that contributes to Richard's loss of the throne in the first place.

EXERCISES

1. Consider one of the plays you are studying. In what way is language used to create the sort of mood and atmosphere that may be said to dominate the play?
2. Examine the ways in which diction and manner of expression is used to suggest deep insights into the protagonist in one of the plays you are studying.
3. Read the following soliloquy from *Hamlet* and then answer the questions below:

> O, that this too too solid flesh would melt,
> Thaw, and resolve itself into a dew!
> Or that the Everlasting had not fix'd
> His canon 'gainst self-slaughter! O God! O God!
> How weary, stale, flat, and unprofitable
> Seem to me all the uses of this world!
> Fie o't! O fie! 'tis an unweeded garden,
> That grows to seed; things rank and gross in nature
> Possess it merely.

(a) How would you describe Hamlet's state of mind here?

(b) Which three words or phrases best convey Hamlet's disgust with life?

(c) How would you describe the type of language and imagery used here?

4. Read the following opening speech of Volpone as he gazes at his store of gold, then answer the questions below:

> Hail the world's soul, and mine! more glad than is
> The teeming earth to see the long'd-for sun
> Peep through the horns of the celestial Ram,
> Am I, to view thy splendour darkening his;
> That lying here, amongst my other hoards,
> Show'st like a flame by night, or like the day
> Struck out of chaos, when all darkness fled
> Unto the centre. O thou son of Sol[1]
> But brighter than thy father, let me kiss,
> With adoration, thee, and every relic[2]
> Of sacred treasure in this blessed room.

[1]the sun
[2]holy artefact

(a) How would you describe the language of this extract? In what ways is it poetic? In what ways is it shocking?

(b) What insights are offered by this language into the nature of the speaker?

CHAPTER 8

SPECTACLE AND MUSIC

Doctor Johnson felt that Drama had to *entertain* to succeed. What is meant by entertainment in this sense is clearly something which pleasingly and satisfyingly engages our mind and heart in a deeper manner than something which pleasantly passes an hour or two and is forgotten. This element of pleasure is crucial to all art forms, yet Drama, with its potential for physical spectacle, perhaps starts with a distinct advantage.

One need only observe the faces of young children at a circus, or pantomime, to glimpse the basic human love of *spectacle*. Similarly, there is a sense of almost child-like anticipation and delight amongst a theatre audience at that magical moment when the house-lights dim, the curtain rises and the decorated stage is lit before us. We never quite lose this sense of wonder, no matter how many performances we might attend, even of the same play. We eagerly await the "feast" for our eyes as much as that for our ears, minds and hearts.

We might tend to feel that the contemporary theatre—laser lighting, holographs, revolving stages and all—is far more spectacular than that of previous ages. Yet spectacle is far more than surface glitter. It relates to the sweep and flow of the action, the appearance and "presence" of the characters on the stage and the rich worlds created by the images of the play's language as much as (if not more than) it does to impressive technical effects of lighting, sets, costume and make-up. Audience expectations as to what constitutes spectacle are, in any case, relative to the conditions of the theatre of the age. A play like *Antony and Cleopatra* would have been as spectacular to its original audience as a present-day performance, with all the advantages of the modern theatre, might appear to us today.

A *spectacle* may be defined as *a show or display, designed for public attention, curiosity, or admiration*. The dramatist can never forget the element of "display". His earliest thoughts on how the play is to be composed, the material arranged, will automatically and constantly involve envisaging the play as it will appear on stage. Yet a balance must be achieved. Character, action and language must be "spectacular" enough to promote and sustain audience interest, without becoming over-spectacular. If the dramatist strives too hard for the sensational, he is likely to detract from the overall harmony and unity and natural development of the entire play.

For the dramatist, spectacle will involve the visually striking elements of character and situation. Such touches need not be overtly spectacular in the more modern sense. The sumptuous court of Cleopatra, the stage presence of Othello, or Lear, the pastoral Forest of Arden, the magical world of *Midsummer Night's Dream*, or *The Tempest*, the final scene of *Doctor Faustus*, the climax of *The White Devil*, Bluntschli's dramatic entrance in *Arms and the Man*, the trial scene in *The Crucible*—these are all obvious instances of *dramatic* spectacle. More subtle, yet equally impressive in visual terms, are the elemental, barren settings of *King Lear's* heath and the similar setting of *Waiting for Godot*, the lonely, agonised contemplation of Hamlet, the domestic squalor and chaos of *Look Back in Anger* and Hedda Gabler, lying dead in the midst of her seemingly safe and secure middle-class home and artefacts.

MUSIC

Aristotle included music in his list of essential dramatic components because it was an integral part of Greek Drama. It has sustained its importance in the development of Drama, but we must here distinguish between four *strands* of music in Drama. The first three strands will not concern the student of English Literature directly, for here the musical element is expanded into equal (if not superior) status with the other aspects of Drama. The first, most obviously, is *opera*—now an autonomous art form in its own right. The second is *music drama*, such as the collaborations of the dramatist Brecht and the composer Weill in *The Threepenny Opera*. The third is the so-called *musical*, which perhaps grew out of the extremely popular "light" opera of Gilbert and Sullivan and became, itself, immensely popular in America in the thirties, forties and fifties—and still enjoys considerable popularity today.

What will be of interest to the student is the *occasional* use of music in an otherwise "standard" dramatic work. Used in this way, music can be most effective in enhancing the atmosphere or emotion of a specific scene or incident. Few dramatists actually attempt such a specialist facility, yet Shakespeare uses music extensively. He explored its potential in comedy—both in the light, often ribald, songs of the "clown" figures in the earlier comedies and, in more sinister fashion, in Iago's comic song at the victory celebration and the Fool's ditties in *King Lear*. Music is used to create a sense of pathos and impending tragedy by Ophelia and Desdemona. It is used to emphasise the harmony and optimism at the "wedding" resolution to the comedies. Yet perhaps the most creative and striking uses Shakespeare made of music lie in the way it is featured to enhance an atmosphere of mystery and dream—as in *The Tempest*, or that strange, evocative scene in *Antony and Cleopatra*, where the soldiers hear "strange music" in the air and under the ground, as Antony's "protective god" finally abandons him.

EXERCISES

1. What do you understand by the term "dramatic spectacle"? What are the most striking examples of dramatic spectacle in the plays you are studying?
2. Consider an important scene in one of the plays you are studying. Imagine you are a director concerned with staging that scene. Describe what your set would look like, how your characters would appear on the stage (i.e. costume, make-up, etc.) and what lighting you would use, along with any other "devices" or "touches" you can think of, to make the scene as *visually* striking as possible.
3. Do any of the plays you are studying make use of music? If so, how and why is it used? If not, consider one or two scenes that might benefit from the addition of music—indicating the type of music that would be most effective and giving reasons for selecting such scenes.

CHAPTER 9

THE DEVELOPMENT
OF DRAMA

Any course of study of a specific play will be considerably enriched by a general awareness of the development of Drama as a whole. Our understanding and appreciation of a play increases when we see it against the background traditions in Drama that prevailed both before and during the time the play was written. In other areas of literature, "period" labels (Romantic, Augustan, Victorian, etc.) have only the most limited and superficial usefulness. However, with Drama, such generalised categorisation has a greater validity and relevance. This is because the type of theatre of any given age (i.e. its physical structure, conventions, facilities, etc.) will be common to all the dramatists of that age—and the type of theatre will very much influence the type of Drama produced. In this sense, a term such as Restoration Comedy will be far more meaningful than, say, Romantic Poetry: the work of Congreve and Wycherley will share far greater similarities than the poems of Keats, Shelley, Wordsworth and Byron.

The following is a broad outline of the development of Drama. It will provide the necessary background against which any individual play may be related. This will indicate how that play developed as part of the evolving tradition, as well as highlighting its unique individuality within that tradition.

Earliest Origins

"The theatre," said Matthew Arnold, "is irresistible." If this is the case, it could well result from Aristotle's belief that there is a natural and compelling human instinct for *imitation*. Again, we have only to watch young children to sense the possible truth of this proposition. Yet while all art seeks to "imitate" life in some sense, none does so as forcefully or *literally* (i.e. physically) as Drama.

The origins of Drama seem to have stemmed from this desire to imitate. They are found in ancient rituals and religious celebrations, where human beings would "imitate" the gods, seeking perhaps to gratify them and influence their future actions towards their human "subjects". Dramatic ritual is still very much a feature of many religions across the world today.

Greek Drama

The birthplace of Western Drama, as a form of art in its own right, was Ancient Greece, although we still find a strong "religious" element here, as Greek Drama concerns itself exclusively with myths and legends of the gods and Fate.

Before we can appreciate the Drama of any age, we must first understand the conventions and implications of the type of *theatre* in which it took place. This is particularly true with Greek Drama, as the theatrical environment which helped shape the actual Drama was so very different from our own. Greek plays were performed in the open air, at certain annual festivals, all "religious" in some sense. Audiences attended such performances not only to be entertained, but also with the sense of taking part in a form of worship and religious obligation.

The actors were all male and wore elaborate masks, the significance of each one already being known to the audience. No violent or "dramatic" action was allowed (literally "allowed", as the plays were initially submitted as part of a competition and had to conform to certain rules). There was no curtain, scenery or costume, other than simple goatskins. Most significant events and actions took place "off-stage" and were reported back to the main actors by the Chorus. The Chorus was an essential feature of Greek Drama—a group of actors, constantly on stage, who would draw the attention of the audience to the crucial parts of the play and comment upon their significance. The main attention, therefore, was focused on the speakers and their reactions rather than incident and movement.

As the basic story of the play would already be familiar to the audience, this absence of direct action allowed that audience to concentrate fully on what is, quite simply, the essence of all Drama: the thoughts and emotions of human beings at times of great stress, pressure and conflict. This helps to explain the continuing appeal of Greek Drama to the present day. It remains a profound dramatic experience rather than a period-piece curiosity.

The final feature of Greek Theatre is that all plays were performed "in the round"—i.e. in a central arena, with the audience surrounding the entire stage. This is a device to which many twentieth-century plays have returned with great effect. (Other aspects of Greek Theatre have also had such modern adaptations. One thinks especially of T.S. Eliot's use of the Chorus in *Murder in the Cathedral*.)

Once we understand the nature of Greek Theatre, we can see how this has affected the nature of Greek Drama. Originally, this meant only tragedy; comedy developed later in plays where the religious element was reduced. Greek Tragedy is formal, poetic, solemn and static. The delivery of lines was closer to public recitation and oratory than "acting" as we understand it. Plays would centre on the dilemma facing the main character and usually resulted in his or her death. The *Oresteia* of Aeschylus, Euripides' *Medea*, and the *Oedipus Rex* and *Antigone* of Sophocles probably represent the highest achievements of Greek Tragedy. Here is an example, (taken from *Antigone*,) of the sort of sombre, dignified and powerful tone to be found in such plays:

> Then hear this. Ere the chariot of the sun
> Has rounded once or twice his wheeling way,
> You shall have given a son of your own loins
> To death, in payment for death—two debts to pay:
> One for the life that you have sent to death,
> The life you have abominably entombed;
> One for the dead still lying above ground
> Unburied, unhonoured, unblest by the gods below.
> You cannot alter this. The gods themselves
> Cannot undo it.

Greek Comedy comes from a word meaning merry-making and, in stark contrast to Greek Tragedy, evolved as a robust, vigorous, lively, occasionally lyrical (though more often abusive and even vulgar) satiric commentary on human weakness—especially in the hands of an Aristophanes.

ROMAN DRAMA

As in most matters cultural and philosophical, the Romans contented themselves with imitating Greek Drama rather than striving for any particular originality of their own. Perhaps the only serious development lies in the work of Seneca. Seneca established the "five act" format, which actually enjoyed an amazingly long life as the standard format of all Drama (some seventeen hundred years!) . Other innovations found in Seneca are a more elaborate use of language, the use of ghosts and magic, and the concept of the "confidant". His plays are mainly concerned with the *stoic acceptance of Fate*, yet they also focus strongly on the concept of *revenge*—thus establishing a theme that will be central to Drama for centuries to come.

MEDIEVAL DRAMA

The earliest Drama actually in English is found in the Middle Ages. This looks back somewhat to Greek Drama, in that medieval plays are virtually all religious. However, there are significant developments in terms of "spectacle"—with movement, action, costume and props. The actors are still entirely male, yet they no longer wear masks. They are also required to *act* as opposed to *reciting* their parts. A play would often be performed in sections; a procession of carts decorated with rudimentary scenery would travel through the town; the leading cart would enact the first scene at a particular stopping-point, then move on to the second "venue" and be replaced by the second cart and scene. At each vantage point, the audience would gradually see the play pass before its eyes, quite literally. There were essentially three types of medieval Drama.

Mystery Plays

These were based on Biblical themes, especially the Nativity of Christ, the Passion and the Resurrection. They were often most ambitious in the scope they attempted—sometimes Man's entire spiritual history (in Christian terms), from the Creation to the day of Judgement. (Such complexity led to the plays being performed in the segmented "cycles" we have just mentioned. On occasions, the performance would be spread over several days and involve vast numbers of actors. The Mystery Play tends to compensate for a lack of subtlety in thought, language and characterisation by providing the broad sweep of ambitious and varied spectacle.

Miracle Plays

Such plays were mainly concerned with the lives of the saints and the Virgin Mary. However, while the Mystery Play would adhere quite closely to its Biblical material, the Miracle Play took greater creative licence with its subject-matter. The performance was the same as for the Mystery Play, yet the Miracle Play would move steadily towards the actual "miracle" around which the entire play was centred. This automatically instilled a sense of *climax* into the action. The careful preparation for an effective climax makes the Miracle Play a far more "dramatic" experience than that of the Mystery Play; the latter was obliged to be completely faithful to its original material and could not arrange that material for the greatest dramatic impact. As such, the Mystery Play is likely to have sensational climaxes—the Creation, the Flood, the birth of Christ, the Crucifixion, etc.—occurring virtually haphazardly all over the place.

Morality Plays

These were an interesting development a little later in the medieval period. They were more self-contained, precise and intense than the sprawling Mystery Play. They focused on the eternal struggle between good and evil for the human soul. Thought, theme and idea become more important than spectacle. The characters tend to be one-dimensional personifications of particular virtues and vices (Anger, Chastity, Sloth, Pride, etc.), yet they are vigorously and dramatically presented. The classic example, and one which is still performed today, is *Everyman*, which looks at the perils and temptations of evil we all face in the journey through life.

Morality Plays are basically extended allegories—where a moral issue is offered to the audience in a physical representation. The intention was to instruct the audience as to what constituted moral behaviour, yet in spite of the close links with Christian morality, the plays are no longer "tied" to Biblical and liturgical writings and models. For this reason, the Morality Play forms an important first step in the development of Drama as a means of creative communication in its own right—completely free and independent in its choice and use of material.

One other type of medieval Drama deserves attention. This came much later and was entirely secular (i.e. non-religious). It was the *Commedia Dell' Arte*, which was developed in Italy but soon became immensely popular across Europe. Professional actors, sometimes using masks, or even puppets, would travel the land presenting improvised plays around stock situations and characters. This introduces two important dramatic concepts. *Improvisation* is where the actors perform without a script. This allows the skilled performer tremendous scope in responding to the particular audience before him. He may tease, or cajole, a quiet, unresponsive audience, or go to outlandish extremes with an enthusiastic and captive one. Each performance is modified and tailored to suit each audience and is therefore unrepeatable and unique. At the other extreme, stock characters and situations are unsubtle, simplified, even clichéd, and already highly familiar to the audience.

Combining the "improvised" and the "stock", the classic situation of the *Commedia* would involve the foolish old Jealous Husband returning unexpectedly to find the Faithless Wife and the Young Adventurer in a highly compromising position—stock characters in a time-worn, "stock scene". The improvisation will then take over with the ingenuity with which the young man seeks to extricate himself from the delicate and dangerous situation; the more outrageous, implausible and unlikely the "explanation", the more the audience will enjoy the performance.

The *Commedia Dell' Arte* exercised a huge influence on Renaissance and Elizabethan Drama. Its robust, energetic, frequently crude and irreverent farce completes the movement of Drama away from religion. Indeed, anything less solemn, devout, or religious than the *Commedia* would be difficult to imagine.

ELIZABETHAN DRAMA

This age sees the first true flowering of English Drama. It is also the earliest age that will be of specific and detailed interest to the student of Advanced Level English Literature. Again, it is necessary to look at the "theatre" of the age before considering its Drama.

Plays are now presented in specially constructed theatres—the first being built in 1576, though they are still essentially "open air". These theatres were extremely popular, especially the Globe, built by

Shakespeare's company in 1599. However, now that Drama was secular, it was not considered respectable and all the theatres were therefore situated outside the city limits of London, on the South Bank of the Thames. (The Puritans considered Drama so immoral that they closed down all the theatres.)

The stage itself was a large, uncurtained platform that extended out into the "pit" where the "groundlings", or poorer spectators, would stand on three sides of the stage. Around the sides of the building were tiers, or "galleries", where the wealthier patrons would sit. A roof, known as the "shadow", or "heavens", projected out over part of the stage to protect the actors from the elements. This also allowed certain props and devices to be lowered onto the stage as part of the dramatic action. There was no scenery and only basic props to suggest the set— a bed, a throne, a tree, etc. Such props were there to symbolise the setting rather than to realistically represent it. The actors, however, might now wear elaborate costumes. Once again, the cast would be entirely male.

At the rear of the stage was an inner area, separated from the main section by a curtain. This was known as the "alcove" or "study" and might be used to indicate a bedroom or some other private space. Above the alcove was the "upper stage", or "chamber", which would serve for any elevated location—like the battlements of a castle, or Juliet's famous balcony.

The implications of such a theatre were important. There are now three acting areas, which allows for more movement and variation in the presentation. Yet the most significant influence of the Elizabethan Theatre on Elizabethan Drama is found in the way a seemingly negative drawback is turned into the most positive (and, in retrospect, characteristic) element. The complete absence of scenery made the stage a neutral, undefined territory. It could, quite simply, become any place the dramatist chose to make it—and, with no sets or scenery to change, could just as quickly become "somewhere else". Yet a sense of location and atmosphere are crucial to effective Drama. The only way this could be achieved in such a theatre was through the power of language. The words themselves must create the scene, the location and (with the absence of lighting) the time of day or night. As a result, Elizabethan Drama produced some of the finest passages of descriptive poetry in English. An audience may have been huddled together on a cold, bleak early winter afternoon in London, yet once a speech such as Romeo's "But soft! What light through yonder window breaks?" gathers its momentum, they are transported to the glimmering warmth of a Veronese dawn.

The variable acting areas and freedom from restrictions of fixed sets and cumbersome scenery produced a great sweep of movement and fluidity of action in the finest Elizabethan Drama. Although most plays at this time are still somewhat "formal" (and written in verse), there is a greater degree of realism than before; characters and actions appear more "natural". However, it is interesting to note that Shakespeare, ever the *practical* dramatist, writes stylised love-scenes. The passion is always in the language, never the action. With young boys playing the female roles, Shakespeare would not risk losing the dramatic tension of an emotional scene by having some groundling wag commenting out loud about Cleopatra's pubescent bristles and stubble.

Elizabethan Drama is also characterised by its great variety. This is found not only from play to play, but even within individual works. The theatre was becoming a commercially attractive investment, yet, as we have noted already, the dramatist lives by "pleasing" his audience. The Elizabethan audience was as socially diverse as it is possible to imagine, with aristocrats and intellectuals in the galleries and uneducated apprentices in the pit. Plays frequently attempted to encompass edifying and serious moral and philosophical issues for the gallery and sensational action and broad humour for the "groundlings". This accounts for the seemingly inappropriate presence of the various "clown" figures in some of Shakespeare's most sombre tragedies (although the dramatist develops their presence as part of the unified scheme). The groundlings expected their clown "by right" and would soon vent their displeasure if he was absent from the action. In Shakespeare's company, Will Kemp was an early "superstar" in his own right as a clown and the dramatist had constant difficulties in restraining Kemp from improvising beyond the script in search of titillating the audience on his own. The prospect of England's leading literary giant arguing endlessly with a self-willed, egotistic "clown" may appear humorous, yet the problem was serious. Hamlet's warning to the actors to "stick to the text" is often felt to be a pointed and personal "memo" from Shakespeare to Kemp.

A final, general observation on Elizabethan Drama is also related to audience expectation. There was a growing popularity at the time for "sensational" Drama. Given the financial rewards now possible from a successful production, dramatists tended to fuel this element all the more. This currying to popular demand is always a danger. In our own times, advances in technology have led theatre and film audiences to expect all sorts of ingenious and astounding "special effects", to thrill "as never before". This in turn has spawned the present spate of horror and science fiction fantasies. For the Elizabethans, the prevalent taste was for gory, bloody Revenge plays, modelled on Seneca, yet far outstripping him in terms of violent language and action. If the finest Elizabethan dramatists managed to transcend the current preference, they were still obliged to cater for, and attract, an audience with such expectations. As such, the "sensational" element is never far from the surface. Most would regard *King Lear* as a timeless masterpiece—a philosophic, poetic and powerfully moving portrayal of the potential tragedy inherent in Man's very existence. Yet even here we find an intense violence of language and an outrageous piece of Revenge sensationalism—the blinding of Gloster. In a very real sense, every Shakespearean tragedy is rooted in the tradition of the Revenge play.

Apart from Shakespeare, whom we will look at separately later, there are two other outstanding Elizabethan dramatists. Christopher Marlowe was himself something of an influence on Shakespeare. His finest work is characterised by the sort of rich language we noted earlier in the passage from *Doctor Faustus*. Indeed, English blank verse tragedy reaches its first real pinnacle in Marlowe's work. Although not above sensational and cruel incident, Marlowe's best plays are carried forward by highly developed protagonists, men of immense character, sweeping passion and splendid poetry. *Doctor Faustus* is the first real *psychological* play on the English stage. It is a new departure in tragedy as it examines, in intimate and perceptive detail, the struggle of a great personality doomed to ultimate failure by his own human limitations.

Ben Jonson, like Marlowe, adopts a largely "classical" approach to Drama, yet his vastly different temperament produces vastly different plays. Although Jonson wrote tragedy, he is chiefly remembered for vigorous and sharp comic satire. *Volpone* and *The Alchemist* stand unrivalled in English Drama as powerful attacks on greed, materialism and gullibility. The characters bristle with comic liveliness and invention, the action rattles along with controlled and structured speed and the language evocatively captures the subterranean world of London "lowlife", with all its racy colloquialism.

There are two other dramatists of note. Thomas Kyd's *The Spanish Tragedy* is almost a prototype for the standard Elizabethan Revenge tragedy. Although the play has its psychologically acute moments, it is largely Senecan drama in even more lurid dress. Similarly, Tourneur's *The Revenger's Tragedy*, has a title which instantly indicates identical preoccupations. Certainly it is an impressive dramatic experience, yet one that is ultimately limited by its gloom, pessimism and violence.

Jacobean Drama

Although the actual Drama of this age produces little of lasting significance, there are several important developments concerning the theatre. These arose primarily because the theatre moved "indoors". This
immediately alters the nature of the dramatic presentation (for the
dramatist) and the dramatic experience (for the audience). The whole
process now becomes more intimate, closed, intense and concentrated.
There are now considerations of scenery and rudimentary lighting. The
fluidity of the Elizabethan theatre is replaced by the *sophistication* of the
indoor theatre. Shakespeare himself, at the end of his career, mirrors
this change. The final two plays, *The Winter's Tale* and *The Tempest*, performed at the indoor Blackfriars Theatre, have a distinct "masque"
element and are very different in tone and nature from the plays
written for the outdoor Globe.

James I was a great patron and lover of the theatre, yet however
appealing Jacobean Drama may have been to its contemporaries, few of
its achievements have stood the test of the time. Webster's *The White
Devil* and *The Duchess of Malfi* are certainly powerful and worthy Revenge plays, yet, by and large,they tend to neglect character and thought
for sensational effect. The plays and collaborations of Beaumont and
Fletcher were extremely popular in their own day, but now appear
somewhat light, superficial and "mannered", catering exclusively to an
elitist, at times effete, audience.

Restoration Drama

Between 1642 and 1660 theatres were closed in Cromwell's England.
With the restoration of Charles II, however, theatres were quickly re-
opened or re-built to satisfy immense popular demand. Again there
were developments in the physical arrangement of the theatre that
imposed new demands and challenges on the dramatists. Now nearly
all the audience was seated. A curtain was draped across the main part
of the stage. The stage was neutral, unspecific territory no longer; with
the use of scenery and lighting, it became a precisely located time and
place that lent a more realistic or naturalistic backdrop to the characters
and their actions. Elaborate and poetic descriptions of place, so pronounced in Elizabethan Drama, now virtually disappear from English

Drama. The move towards greater realism had one further significant advance at this time. In Restoration Drama, female roles are, for the first time, played by actual females—thus replacing the generations of men and boys who had struggled so (wo)manfully for centuries before them.

This obviously had a marked influence on the way dramatists now envisaged their female creations. These tended to be played down in the past (even allowing for such marvellous creations as Lady Macbeth and the Duchess of Malfi) for fear, on the dramatist's part, of straining the illusion of females being portrayed by males. (With considerable pragmatic ingenuity, Shakespeare's usual response to this problem, in nearly all the comedies, is to have the "woman" dressed as a boy for most of the play. Critics have made much of such role reversal, in terms of philosophical examinations into the search for true identity, role expectations and male and female "principles". It may well be all of these things, yet it is also an undeniably clever piece of stage-craft!)

The use of actresses in Restoration Drama obviously encouraged dramatists to look more closely at the potential of female roles. This in turn began the great tradition of leading female characters. We find this almost immediately with Congreve's Lady Wishfort.

Restoration Drama evolved a particular brand of witty, satirical, often bawdy comedy. This perfectly captured the excesses to be found in English society, a period of considerable indulgence after the severe moral restrictions of the Puritans. Such comedy is sometimes known as Comedy of Manners, where the main focus is on Man's behaviour as a social animal. Congreve's *The Way of the World* provides a series of satiric observations around this theme, an exposure of the spectacularly licentious groups who inhabited the courts of the Restoration. Wycherley's *The Country Wife* is a similar, though coarser and more robust, attack on fortune-hunting, lewdness and the search for social prestige.

A criticism often levelled at Restoration Comedy is that the wickedness is portrayed in such seemingly joyous detail—with the dramatists and audience alike taking an almost salacious pleasure in it—that the moral purpose of the intended satire is lost. Such plays are so resplendent with comic life and detail, that they seem more a celebration of wickedness than a condemnation. This may be the case with lesser dramatists, but with the masterly Congreve and Wycherley, the satiric purpose shines clearly through.

Farquhar also shows a facility for vigorous language and pungent satire. He also introduced an even greater degree of "realism" than was fashionable at the time, yet plays like *The Recruiting Officer* and *The Beaux Stratagem* lack the cutting-edge of Congreve and Wycherley and also incline towards the sentimental. Away from comedy, Dryden offers a form of tragedy where the grand, "heroic" element is pared down both in character and simplified language.

Although not a figure of the Restoration proper, the plays of Sheridan at the end of the eighteenth century owe much in spirit to their immediate predecessors. *The School for Scandal* and *The Rivals*, however, offer the satiric exposure of Restoration Comedy together with an increased sophistication of wit and a clearer moral tone. The situations in these plays may by now be familiar, yet they are treated with freshness and ingenuity. Both plays also reveal a considerable development in the sense of theatrical effect, especially such scenes as the interview between Sir Anthony Absolute and his son in *The Rivals* and the auction scene in *The School for Scandal*. There is a genial mockery of affectation (Lydia Languish) and the glorious comic creation of Mrs Malaprop in *The Rivals*. *The School for Scandal* resembles Restoration satire the more closely, yet Lady Teazle is a much more refined and sophisticated creation than Mrs Pinchwife in *The Country Wife*.

NINETEENTH CENTURY DRAMA

Coming after the achievements of Restoration Drama, and given the significant developments in the theatre itself, the Drama of the following age is surprisingly disappointing. This "decline" was a matter of serious concern and argument for the writers and critics of the time. On the whole, we find only a motley collection of sensational melodrama, superficial farce and over-elaborate (and frequently "unstageable") verse dramas.

Towards the end of the century, however, a revival began to take shape. Significantly, the main influence for the renaissance of serious Drama came not from England, but from Norway. Henrik Ibsen is often regarded as the father of modern Drama. Plays such as *A Doll's House, Hedda Gabler, Ghosts* and *Peer Gynt* were to exert a profound influence across Europe and later America. Ibsen's plays are often referred to as the "drama of ideas" and here we find the dramatist addressing himself to serious moral issues and the complexity of social relationships. There are two distinctive features of Ibsen's plays—the strand of *social realism* and the haunting use of *poetic symbolism*. He is able to combine skilful mastery of dramatic technique with penetrating insight into character. The themes, ideas, lessons and moral persuasion of these plays unfold naturally against the sombre, dark, often claustrophobic background of isolated, provincial Norwegian towns. Yet the universal themes and realities that Ibsen deals in transcend the narrow confines of his settings and the plays remain compelling, disconcerting and relevant studies of the human condition. This is the essence of all true Drama; the individual play is necessarily rooted in a specific time and place—and this very setting may well be of great interest in its own right, either as a mirror into our own times, or as an insight into different times and places. Yet the main issues of the play—what we have already termed the *psychological realism*, whereby it captures the essences of human life—relate to all people, at all times, in all places.

The first major English dramatist to benefit from the influence of Ibsen was George Bernard Shaw. Here again we find a "drama of ideas", as Shaw explores the philosophical, religious and social issues of his day. Shaw took risks with this extent of seriousness in Drama. His appeal is to the intellect rather than the emotions; thought.is more important than action. We have noted that the dramatist must "please" in some way, yet Shaw's plays not only presented serious issues, they presented issues which Shaw himself designated unpleasant (prostitution, slum landlordism, war as grim reality and not heroic fantasy, etc.). Such plays also ran counter to the popular preference for light Victorian melodrama. Yet *Arms and the Man, Saint Joan, Major Barbara* and *Man and Superman* still managed to appeal by virtue of their sophisticated wit and eloquent expression. The emphasis on thought and language makes Shaw one of the least "dramatic" and most *literary* of playwrights—one to be read as much as viewed. The plays themselves contain extended prefaces, character descriptions and stage directions which, rather than offering technical assistance, form an integral part of the play's overall intention.

In terms of temperament and philosophy, the other leading dramatist at the turn of the century could almost have come from a different planet from George Bernard Shaw. Oscar Wilde was the archetypal aesthete who believed that art should be above the petty concerns of daily life and exist solely "for its own sake". Whereas Shaw concerns himself with political and social idealism, with "thought" and "idea", Wilde's main focus is on style and presentation. Structure is everything and the more ornate and elaborate the presentation of that structure (i.e. the plot) then the more admirably "artistic" the creation. In two of Wilde's finest plays, *Lady Windermere's Fan* and *The Importance of Being Earnest*, character and situation are entirely improbable—yet Wilde never believed that Art should be "probable", in the terms of our own daily world; Art creates its own world and the dramatist need only be faithful to, and consistent in, his portrayal of that world. One important characteristic is shared with Shaw—the reliance on wit and humour. Yet with Wilde we return more to the "feel" of Restoration Comedy, for the wit itself, the elegance of expression, the style and dexterity of the theatrical presentation—these are everything.

Although so different temperamentally, Shaw and Wilde both held their respective beliefs so forcefully in their lives and works that both suffered considerable periods of unpopularity with their contemporaries. However, their dramatic achievements and influence have long outlasted the prejudices of their own age; and if Shaw's intentions were the more serious and humanitarian, it is Wilde's *The Importance of Being Earnest* that stands as the one truly "classic" creation of the age in its particular dramatic genre.

In more subtle terms, the influence of Ibsen emerges again in the work of Synge. As with Ibsen, we find, in plays such as *The Playboy of the Western World*, an accomplished piece of dramatic structure offering perceptive insights into a specific, "enclosed", rural community. The play also unfolds a rich vein of poetic symbolism that evokes the peasantry of Ireland as hauntingly as Ibsen captures the bourgeoisie of Norway. Nothing like Synge's major play had ever before been seen on the British stage—so much so that its first performance, at the Abbey Theatre in Dublin, actually prompted rioting amongst the audience. Synge completes this curious revival of Drama in English, founded on an initially Norwegian influence, and carried forth by three great dramatists with pronounced (though very different) Irish connections.

TWENTIETH CENTURY DRAMA

As in the previous century, English Drama at this time was again heavily influenced by a foreign playwright. Bertolt Brecht evolved a theory of Drama that had a profound impact on his contemporaries and immediate successors. Whether they felt in sympathy with Brecht's ideas and sought to develop them, or whether, they disagreed and attempted new directions, most dramatists of the present century felt obliged to "relate" to the Brecht position in one way or another.

In the thirties and forties, Brecht worked on the concept and practice of "epic" theatre. This sought to revert the trend towards increasing "naturalism" in Drama by creating plays where the audience are deliberately and constantly made aware that they are watching a staged performance. Brecht requires no "willing suspension of disbelief", where an audience pretends they are watching real people in real situations. Plays like *Mother Courage* and *The Caucasian Chalk Circle* consciously distance the audience from the characters and the action. The audience is not invited to share the thoughts, feelings and fears of the characters. Instead, Brecht wants his audience "free" to concentrate on the play's overall intention and theme, its philosophical or political message. Brecht feels these over-riding issues are so important that he wants the audience to assess and judge their validity and importance and to do so with their critical faculties clear and undistracted (i.e. by *not* becoming involved in the dramatic action itself). For this reason, Brecht's plays are sometimes termed "theatre of alienation". The audience is kept "outside" the characters and their situations, distanced and "alienated", so that they may dispassionately and impartially observe the *issues* at the centre of the play. Such Drama becomes an extreme (though logical) development of Ibsen's "theatre of ideas", as promoted by Shaw's belief that Drama has a deep responsibility to concern itself with the social, political and philosophical problems of the age. (It also looks back to the distancing effect of Greek Tragedy.)

A similar reaching back into some form of "epic" Drama (though in a different sense) is found in the plays of T.S. Eliot. *Murder in the Cathedral* is an experiment with Verse Drama. *The Cocktail Party* and *The Confidential Clerk* are specifically based on Greek Drama and disguise their serious purpose beneath the standard "drawing-room" comedy so much in vogue between the wars. The language of these plays, deliberately plain and undecorated, is again in verse.

Since World War II, there has been a greater diversification in English Drama. We find the frequently surreal world of Absurd Drama, where the sparse, poignant, "life reduced to barest essentials" productions of Samuel Beckett are the finest examples in English. In the fifties, there was the dramatic explosion of the "angry young men". *Look Back In Anger* and the Wesker trilogy offer powerful explorations of social and political issues from the standpoint of the idealistic individual who is constantly at the mercy of a stultifying, wrong-headed and all-powerful bureaucracy. Most recently, the work of Pinter and Stoppard combines absurdist elements with social comment. Pinter has developed a particularly effective "comedy of menace"—with ambiguous, deceptively casual dialogue, intriguing situation and a fine balance between comedy and strange suspense. Stoppard teases his audience with a seemingly flippant treatment of deep philosophical and psychological themes, bizarre character and situation, and scintillating comic dialogue.

Finally, the student of English Literature should be aware of the leading American dramatists of this century. Eminent among these is Eugene O'Neill. With a relentless sense of tragedy, O'Neill adapted the seriousness of Ibsen into the American theatre, exploring the tormented psyches and relationships of his characters in a range of different dramatic techniques. We find the "naturalism" of *Anna Christie*, the symbolism of *The Hairy Ape* and even updated Greek Tragedy in *Mourning Becomes Electra*. The two master-pieces, however, remain *The Iceman Cometh* and *Long Day's Journey Into Night*.

Arthur Miller has devoted much energy into writing for films, yet his concern for liberal values and individual and social morality produced two fine pieces of stage Drama in *The Death of a Salesman* and *The Crucible*. Tennessee Williams provides emotionally tense plays that observe the ways in which sensitive individuals are destroyed by failure, loneliness and obsessions they cannot fulfil. *The Glass Menagerie*, *A Streetcar named Desire*, *Cat on a Hot Tin Roof* and *Night of the Iguana* are now established as major triumphs of modern American Drama. Edward Albee's *Who's Afraid of Virginia Woolf?* offers a penetrating and searing commentary on contemporary relationships, while *Zoo Story* and *The American Dream* provide broader observations on modern life in America as a whole.

SUGGESTED READING

Antigone, Sophocles
Doctor Faustus, Marlowe
Volpone, Jonson
The White Devil, Webster
The Rivals, Sheridan
Hedda Gabler, Ibsen
Arms And The Man, Shaw
The Importance Of Being Earnest, Wilde
Mother Courage, Brecht
Waiting For Godot, Beckett
Look Back In Anger, Osborne

CHAPTER 10

SHAKESPEARE

Although it is somewhat artificial to isolate Shakespeare from the general development of English Drama, his significance—both in terms of Shakespeare's achievement within that evolving tradition and in terms of examination emphasis for the student—requires individual consideration. What we will be concerned with here is a general perspective of Shakespeare as a practising dramatist. We have already observed the major forms and elements of Drama and may now look at the use the leading practitioner in English Drama makes of them.

SHAKESPEARE AND THE NATURE OF DRAMA

In retrospect, it is all too tempting to glamorise the motives, intentions and even the life of artistic genius. We yearn for the man to match the achievement and create images of the dedicated artist sitting in intense and isolated concentration, penning immortal words for the admiration and delight of posterity. With Shakespeare, however, the most useful image to keep in mind is far more mundane—that of the working playwright; of a man determined to succeed in order to live comfortably from his chosen craft; an artist constantly aware of the needs and expectations of his "customers". From the outset, Shakespeare was completely aware of, and at ease with, the need to "please" and appeal. The young provincial came to London, in the classic sense, to "make his fortune". He quickly grasped the rudiments of the craft that had attracted him and then worked extremely hard at developing his own creativity within that craft (some thirty-seven plays in about twenty-five years).

Aware of the need to "appeal" (for physical as well as artistic survival in the big city), Shakespeare quickly revealed an instinct for the essential elements of the successful dramatic experience—compelling character, exciting action, the sense of conflict, the exploration of universal issues,the poetic potential of "dramatic" language, the use of spectacle, music and clowns. Increasingly, as his art develops, Shakespeare is able to unify all these elements towards the central direction and purpose of the play as a whole.

Like Cleopatra, his plays achieved "infinite variety"—partly due, no doubt, to the diversity of the Elizabethan audience. We might imagine it is easier for a dramatist to appeal to the tastes and preferences of his contemporaries rather than unknown future generations. In a real sense, however, it would have been easier for an Elizabethan dramatist to appeal to the refined taste and educated preferences of future literary *cognoscenti* and "experts", than to be able to please the privileged, educated, aristocratic elite *and* the clamouring, unlettered, lower class apprentices who *all* flocked in great numbers to Shakespeare's Globe Theatre.

It is now generally accepted that Shakespeare wrote thirty-seven plays. To this day, arguments remain as to whether he also wrote, or co-wrote, other plays as well—and even as to whether he was wholly responsible for the writing of his own plays. Such controversy is, perhaps, inevitable with any leading artist. The table opposite, however, with *approximate* dates, may be taken to represent the most accepted sequence of Shakespeare's work.

SHAKESPEARE AND TRAGEDY

In terms of tragedy, Shakespeare begins by giving his audience very much what they wanted and were used to—and then more, in an even more extreme dosage than they might have expected. Shakespeare's first tragedy, *Titus Andronicus* (1593), is very much in the tradition of the blood-thirsty Revenge Play. The play's various delights include

	COMEDIES	TRAGEDIES	HISTORIES
1591			Henry VI, Part I
1592	The Comedy of Errors Two Gentlemen of Verona		Henry VI, Part II Henry VI, Part III
1593	Love's Labour's Lost	Titus Andronicus	Richard III
1594			King John
1595	A Midsummer Night's Dream	Romeo and Juliet	Richard II
1596	Merchant of Venice The Taming of the Shrew		
1597			Henry IV, Part I
1598	Much Ado About Nothing		Henry IV, Part II
1599	As You Like It Merry Wives of Windsor	Julius Caesar	Henry V
1601	Twelfth Night	Hamlet	
1602	Troilus and Cressida All's Well That Ends Well		
1604	Measure for Measure	Othello	
1605		King Lear	
1606		Macbeth	
1607		Timon of Athens Antony and Cleopatra	
1608	Pericles		
1609		Coriolanus	
1610	Cymbeline		
1611	The Winter's Tale		
1611-12	The Tempest		
1613			Henry VIII

murder, execution, physical mutilation and rape. The characters, are as "sensational" as the action, with little development or sophistication. It also includes a crude version of the Black Moor/White Lady relationship—a popular theme at the time, derived from Seneca and Ovid—to which Shakespeare will return with far greater depth and subtlety in *Othello*. This is very much an "apprentice piece", where the dramatist learns the ropes without risking any innovations of his own.

The next tragedy is *Romeo and Juliet*. Even allowing for the play's enduring popularity, it remains another stylised, somewhat sensational piece from a playwright who has yet to achieve full artistic maturity. Yet there are considerable developments from the first tragedy. The revenge theme is handled with greater sophistication; here it is a background influence (the dispute between the Montagues and Capulets, Tybalt's consuming passion for "satisfaction") that shapes the main action, but is not, in itself, the main action. The deaths of the young lovers are not forms of revenge as such—except in the deeper philosophical sense as a punishment to the two families, a "revenge" on revenge (or the desire for revenge), perhaps. Character is more interestingly developed, with the result that we feel genuine compassion and sympathy here, which we rarely do before the horrors of *Titus Andronicus*. Juliet herself is an early triumph, and a marked improvement on the silently suffering Lavinia of the first tragedy. She evolves as a heroine of life and vigour, who seeks to direct events, rather than meekly sink under them. Perhaps the major advance in characterisation is the splendidly individualised nature of the "satellite" minor characters, especially Mercutio, Juliet's Nurse and Friar Lawrence.

The eternally enduring feature of this play, however, lies in the poetic sweep and grandeur of its language. For the first time in Shakespearean tragedy, the poet and the dramatist work in equal partnership. The play abounds with the most sublime touches of delicate or emotional lyricism, poetically atmospheric description and compelling dramatic sharpness. The full force of the poet's instinctive "feel" for language is now being unveiled to delineate character, promote action, create tone and engage an audience's more serious thoughts.

It is perhaps difficult to believe that any dramatist's mere third attempt at tragedy could be a play like *Hamlet*. Here we have a satisfying, integrated and balanced union of character, plot, language and thought. The surface situation offers nothing more than yet another Revenge tragedy, yet here the limitations of the genre are completely transcended.This arises from the depth of insight Shakespeare is able to offer into the main character. Shakespeare refines the sense of conflict; instead of being *external*—in the struggle between Titus and Tamora, or the Capulets and the Montagues—it is now *internal*—in the psychological, moral and emotional dilemma within *Hamlet*. Until the final scene of *Hamlet*, remarkably little actually "happens" for a Revenge Play; apart from the death of Polonius, there is precious little blood and gore. (The death of Ophelia is handled in a stylised, "poetic" manner.) Instead, the play broods almost claustrophobically on the thoughts and emotions that torment Hamlet, which leads to the preponderance of soliloquies to reveal the inner turmoil. Attention is moved from "action" to "character"—and, ironically, the action itself becomes all the more interesting. We wonder more about what Hamlet will do because we are shown, in great detail, his reasons and feelings for doing it—or, more properly, for greater parts of the play, *not* doing it. What we have in *Hamlet* is psychological Drama of a high order—an achievement that led to the very threshold of Shakespeare's finest period of tragic writing.

Much speculation has been given as to why, after a varied career in dramatic writing, Shakespeare should concentrate exclusively on tragedy between 1604 and 1608—and, in particular, the dark, towering tragedies upon which his reputation was established. Many have suggested an event in the dramatist's own life (most probably the death of his son, Hamner—the similarity of whose name to Hamlet has further increased such beliefs) led Shakespeare to concentrate on the tragic aspects of human life. Whatever the reason, Shakespeare is now approaching the height of his dramatic maturity and development and is, perhaps, only *now* ready for the ambitious scope of the tragedies of this time.

Between 1604 and 1606 we have the remarkable achievements of *Othello, Macbeth* and *King Lear*. Although written in close proximity, the three plays are very different and each one lends something new to the development of English Drama as a whole.

Othello displays an unusually close adherence to the Three Unities for Shakespeare. As a result, character, action and language are focused acutely and intensely upon the main issue—the malignant force of evil at work on a noble, yet vulnerable nature. The play contains many striking elements—Othello himself, seen in modern times (perhaps as a result of Eliot's observations) as a more complex creation than was traditional, the demonic and pervasive invention of Iago, the economy and precision of plot, and the rich resonance of language. No other Shakespeare tragedy achieves such a profound sense of *catharsis*. The evil of Iago, the jealousy of Othello and the murder of Desdemona are all profoundly disturbing, even frightening. Yet for all its dark, tragic depth, the play ultimately uplifts. Desdemona's purity and innocence survives intact; her final thought is still her love for Othello. With this ideal of love restored, Othello is happy to die and reunite with Desdemona in a kiss. Love itself survives the fiercest assault destructive evil can provide.

The scope of *Macbeth* broadens to involve the supernatural and the subconscious dimensions of the human condition. It is one of Shakespeare's shortest plays, yet, from the opening lines, it engenders an atmosphere of gloom and terror which remains largely unrelieved to the very end. There is little comfort of catharsis here. The play is dominated by Macbeth and Lady Macbeth, who both provide interesting psychological studies in ambition and guilt. As with *Othello*, however, it is the overall dramatic experience that enthralls the audience; it is only on later reflection that we may delineate the powerful elements of compelling character, taut structure, impassioned (and at times shocking) imagery and breathtaking spectacle.

In *King Lear*, we are taken a step further, with a vast, elemental philosophic and poetic examination of Man's position in the universal scheme of things. At times, the central theme—the power of faith and love to overcome evil—is obscured by the prevalent horror, cruelty and gloom. Yet, as with *Othello* and *Macbeth*, here we have a play with a towering protagonist tormented by internal and external conflict. The sense of character is now so firm that it extends to a host of impressive minor characters who are able to develop the sense of conflict to immense proportions. The action moves relentlessly towards profound climax. Again, we have dramatic language of the highest order, fused with poetic power and sharp economy. Spectacle is rich in incident and symbolism to provide a compelling feast for the ears, eyes and hearts and absorbing issues of momentous and universal significance.

It is usual to see a "falling-off" in *Timon of Athens* (1607-8). Certainly Timon's raging against ingratitude and injustice lacks the sublime vehemence of Lear. However, the play probably suffers most by inevitable comparisons with its immediate predecessors. It remains a tense, well-structured tragedy, dominated once more by a magnificent protagonist. Yet the supporting characters are less effectively developed and the fusion of the various dramatic elements less integrated than they are in the three previous tragedies.

SHAKESPEARE AND COMEDY

If there was little that was subtle or refined about Elizabethan tragedy in 1590, there was even less when it came to comedy. For the most part, most plays would contain an attractive pair of lovers, beset by contrived and complex obstacles designed to keep them apart. They depended upon wit, simple characterisation (especially "one-dimensional" villains), speed of action, twist of plot and broad (i.e. slapstick or "knockabout") humour.

Shakespeare again begins by offering the contemporary formula in extreme portions. He adopts the popular device of "disguise" and "mistaken identity" by contriving *two* sets of identical twins in his first comedy, *The Comedy of Errors*. The potential here for "mistaken identity" is virtually inexhaustible! The pace of the action rattles along at a furious rate through the sequence of improbable events, as a jolly, if unmemorable, time is enjoyed by one and all.

The next two attempts show considerable developments in the medium of comedy. *The Taming of the Shrew* shows an increased interest in the potential for more rounded comic character. Petruchio and Kate are light years ahead of the usual naive and simpering lovers that were traditional in comedy at the time.[1] Their gloriously comic exchanges also reveal a new emphasis on a sharper and more incisive use of language for comedy. The "play within a play" concept is another interesting experiment on the dramatist's part. There is still a strong element of unsophisticated farce and many see the play's central "thought" (on the surface, a blunt assertion of female subordination to the male) as heavy-handed and immature. In spite of this potential "offence" to a modern audience (or at least its female contingent), the play has remained a popular part of the Shakespearean repertoire. *Two Gentlemen of Verona* also reveals the sharpened sense of character and melodious use of poetic language. On the whole, though, it is essentially another "light" piece, with a somewhat weak climax.

The next two comedies begin to show what will become the essence of Shakespeare's strength as a comic dramatist, *Love's Labour's Lost* still centres upon a complex, unlikely plot and shallow characterisation, yet the whole issue of love and relationships is now explored with greater depth and sophistication than was common at the time. In Biron, we find a character who will become typical of Shakespeare's more mature creations—a man forced to accept his true self rather than the image he chooses to present of himself to the outside world. This theme is potentially the substance of tragedy, yet Shakespeare is already able to make effective use of it within the broad context of his developing comedy.

Developments in character, theme and language are evident in the next play, *A Midsummer Night's Dream*, where their scope is expanded to include the lyrical and magical world of the supernatural. If *Romeo and Juliet* stands as an early peak of development in *poetic* tragedy, then this play (probably written in the same year) is its equivalent in comedy. Here we explore the range of love from the extremes of self-infatuation to selfless devotion. As with *Romeo and Juliet*, we have a play that has rightly become famous for the haunting lyricism of its dramatic language and an impressive array of "supporting characters".

---

[1] For which reason, they have always been popular roles for actors and actresses.

It is in the plays written between 1597 and 1600 that we find the finest examples of Shakespeare as a writer of comedy. With *The Merchant of Venice*, we are already moving into comedy of a different dimension. Here, the threat of possible tragedy, used in the previous comedies to induce a certain tension into the action, yet never a serious possibility, is developed to create a disconcerting and menacing shadow across most of the play. Character is considerably more detailed and complex. We are not attracted to Shylock, but his character is presented in such depth that we may readily appreciate, perhaps even sympathise with, his feelings. In the end, we are not totally comfortable with the belief that his "punishment" is deserved; in the legal sense, as opposed to humanitarian concerns (of which he himself has received precious little), he has done nothing wrong. The characters we might be expected to admire are deliberately difficult to like. Antonio appears complacent and self-righteous, Bassanio and his friends somewhat smug and superficial—while all of them are unthinkingly bigoted in terms of religious prejudice. Portia is strangely aloof, even cold. This is no longer the light, comic world of simple "black and white" values. Together with this increased "seriousness" of thought and sophisticated characterisation, we find a growing facility for dramatic effect (the court scene) and impressive modulations of dramatic language ("The quality of mercy is not strain'd").[2]

Much Ado About Nothing is precisely that—a rich commentary on the sort of games we play with ourselves and others to allow us to "hide" from our real selves. Throw in a random element of self-seeking evil (Don John) and you have the basic ingredients of tragedy rather than comedy. Yet here, serious issues are handled with a deft, light touch. The two lovers, Beatrice and Benedick, dominate the action from start to finish. However, their "skirmishes of wit" and "merry war of words" are delivered with considerably greater sophistication than those of Petruchio and Kate and basically reveal two characters afraid to face the reality of their true feelings. Disguise is used heavily in this play as a metaphor of this very fact, rather than as an unsubtle device for "quick laughter". There is also a real advance here in Shakespeare's facility with dialogue. Here we sense two people in conversation, interacting, rather than indulging in poetic "set pieces" and talking *at* one another. One of the play's greatest successes lies in this scintillating, inventive repartee between Beatrice and Benedick. Many have seen Restoration Drama as the real forbear of the classic comedy *The*

---

[2] By various estimates, *The Merchant of Venice* is *the* most performed Shakespeare play.

Importance of Being Earnest, yet its true lineage is perhaps more accurately traced to *Much Ado About Nothing*. Dogberry, too, is a rich comic creation. *As You Like It* and *Twelfth Night* probably represent the culmination of Shakespearean comedy.[3] The concept of the positive, vital heroine shaping and directing the play's action, explored to a certain extent in *Love's Labour's Lost* and *The Merchant of Venice*, finds consummate presentation in the vibrant Rosalind and more subtle Viola. The basic format of two lovers struggling to find happiness, fast-paced action, witty dialogue and broad humour through mistaken and misleading identities, is still largely observed—yet now the dramatic experience is much richer and fuller. The pastoral lyricism of the Forest of Arden recalls the magical world of *A Midsummer Night's Dream*, but is now a more satisfying symbol of harmony between the purely human and the purely natural. The protagonists are portrayed with all their attractive virtues *and* humorous foibles. The "villains" impose a serious sense of wickedness, yet are convincingly and finally "won over" by virtue. The central theme of love is explored in the sort of complex depth and detail that makes the final images of harmony more meaningful and satisfying than the standard "happy ending". The plays delight, provoke thought and move with the surest of dramatic control.

SHAKESPEARE AND DARK COMEDY

With these last two plays, it seems that the dramatist has extended the traditional form of comedy as far as possible. The seriousness of the issues looked at in the comedies has been gradually increasing. Shakespeare's developing dramatic technique and vision also seem to have moved beyond the relatively simple world of comedy. The next three comedies, the so-called Dark Comedies or Problem Plays, are of a very different nature. In terms of dramatic complexity, *All's Well That Ends Well* (where it most patently is *not*), *Measure For Measure* (which sounds more like a Revenge play and has many such elements) and the betrayed central relationship of *Troilus and Cressida* all defy neat, simple categorisation as "comedy". They are written at the beginning of

---

[3] I have, perhaps unfairly, chosen to discount *The Merry Wives of Windsor*. The play was hastily contrived at Elizabeth I's request to see Falstaff in love and it remains an unsatisfactory contrivance.

Shakespeare's great "tragic period" and forbode many of the darker elements of those plays. Yet these plays are clearly not intended as tragedies; they have some form of "happy" resolution. Their main preoccupation is again love and relationships—the substance of comedy—yet they are decidedly "unfunny" and much too disconcerting for that label either.

The simplified, idealised world of traditional comedy can no longer accommodate Shakespeare's growing concern for psychological realism. Troilus may well display the extreme behaviour of the comedic lover, yet his doomed relationship with Cressida is, in its own way, poignant and moving. Cressida herself has all the verve and dynamism of a Rosalind, but with a constant and profound (some might say overbalancing) *thought* content. Ulysses offers provoking philosophy on Order and Man's status in the Universal scheme of things. The language of the play is as heavy and demanding as the issues it expresses and as complex as the characters it displays; its dramatic tone and strength approaches that of tragedy:

> This she? no; this is Diomed's Cressida,
> If beauty have a soul, this is not she;
> If souls guide vows, if vows be sanctimonies,
> If sanctimony be the gods delight,
> If there be rule in unity itself,
> This is not she. O madness of discourse,
> That cause sets up with and against itself!
> Bi-fold authority! where reason can revolt
> Without perdition, and loss assume all reason
> Without revolt: this is, and is not, Cressid!

Any humour within the play is acerbic, disconcerting; the affable "clown" is replaced by Thersites—"a deformed and scurrilous Grecian".

What the play does offer is a non-tragic resolution to a complex series of events, characters and ideas. This deepening psychological realism poses problems for the audience expecting conventional Elizabethan comedy, as the audience itself can no longer safely align itself, in terms of moral approval and emotional empathy, with any one set of characters or beliefs. More simplistically stated, there are no obvious heroes or villains. Character, situation, action and idea are offered, quite simply, for observation and consideration—and not for ridicule, approval or instruction, as had become usual in comedy. As in real life, little is now clear-cut, straightforward, black and white.

All's Well That Ends Well is similarly complex in thought and character. There is a subtle difficulty here with the character of Bertram. In a sense, he is a development of Claudio in *Much Ado About Nothing*— one of the play's leading male lovers whom the audience find it extremely difficult to tolerate. This play is darkened by Helena's selfless and suffering devotion to a character so seemingly worthless, although her relationship with the Countess is warm and sustaining. The importance of birth and status to "a worldly match" probably made Bertram less odious, and his behaviour more understandable to the original audiences.

The world of *Measure For Measure* is altogether darker and gloomier. The heroine is still prominent within the action, yet Isabella's fierce defence of her chastity (and at all costs—even to the extent of allowing her brother to die) has an abstract, inhuman coldness to it. It is difficult for the audience to find anyone here they can admire. The ironically named Angelo is a culmination of the male comedy protagonists in Shakespeare who are nearly brought to tragedy by a serious lack of true self-knowledge. He is a twisted mass of neurosis, who finally cracks under the strain of trying to live up to his own self-image of "angelic" purity; having stifled natural instincts all his life, he finally releases them in an unnatural torrent of lust. The Duke eventually resolves the crisis with some form of justice, only after creating such problems himself by a dereliction of duty and indulgently elaborate charades. Mariana, at least, is simply (yet naively) innocent, for which she achieves the dubious "reward" of Angelo. The play as a whole exudes such a prevalent sense of joyless licentiousness and wickedness to which even the bitter, cynical and bawdy humour contributes. This sense of gloom remains unrelieved to the very end—in much the manner of a play like *Macbeth.*

Seen as comedies, these three plays may frustrate and "displease". Yet they are a *new breed* of Drama and require separate classification. In their own unique and original context, they provide intriguing and varied dramatic experiences.

SHAKESPEARE AND THE HISTORIES

Historical Drama was another established form before Shakespeare. Once again, the dramatist rather laboriously finds his way into the genre with a somewhat imitative first attempt—the rather hectic *Henry VI* trilogy.[4] However, here was a form of Drama that quickly proved compatible with Shakespeare's artistic temperament and technique. The basic attraction is perhaps similar to what we have just observed with the Dark Comedies. Although Historical Drama might tend to deal with the more significant and momentous historical characters and events, it also provides the possibility of presenting life with a considerable degree of psychological realism—i.e. neither wholly, nor exclusively, comic or tragic. By concentrating mainly on the lives of certain English kings, the Histories also allow Shakespeare to present, in dramatic terms, one of the main contemporary issues—the different ideas and philosophies surrounding the concept of the "true" leader or monarch.

The first major history, *Richard III*, is, however, designed largely for the "popular" market. The events leading to Richard's rise to power and final overthrow satisfy all the requirements of Revenge plays. The whole question of Richard's implication in the murder of his nephews was still a topical piece of intrigue from recent history. The play succeeds largely through the powerful presence of the brooding protagonist; no other character is seriously developed in the entire play. It is a "static" type of Drama in terms of character, though there is a sweep of spectacle behind the incident and action. The play's formal, at times powerfully resonant, language ("This jewel", "My horse, my horse") is essentially poetic rather than dramatic.

By the time of the next history, important developments appear. In *Richard II*, the protagonist is presented in considerable depth and in language that is more strictly dramatic (i.e. that lends colour, shade and insight into character). A genuine dramatic tension and conflict is established between Richard and Bolingbroke, not only in what they are, but also in what they represent. The central dilemma of the play's "thought"—the "morality" of a more capable, yet unentitled, ruler usurping the rightful, yet ineffectual king—is kept constantly before us. It is further complicated by subtle implications; Bolingbroke's unattractive "earthiness" as opposed to Richard's poetic charm, the former's grudge-bearing sense of grievance and the latter's superficial susceptibility to flattery; and it clashes head-on in both men's overpowering concept of their own worth. Poetic language is still prominent, but is now integrated dramatically as a technique to shade

[4] These three plays are full of action and eloquent verse but completely lack variety of pace, mood and tone. There is little relief from the endless procession of crime and intrigue.

Richard's character and deepen the conflict with Bolingbroke's bluntness. The play moves with a steady rhythm and purpose towards its neatly structured climax and resolution. Many history plays inevitably leave a feeling of "loose ends"—i.e. the known, yet untreated, events that are to happen later. *Richard II* stands as a carefully crafted, unified and complex piece in its own right and marks the initial high platform from which greater achievements will come that we already noted with *Romeo and Juliet* and *A Midsummer Night's Dream* in terms of the tragedies and comedies.[5]

The two parts of *Henry IV* represent some of Shakespeare's finest dramatic writing before the great tragedies. The main characters are developed and presented with deepening psychological insight—indeed, the intriguing complexity of Hal's character is sustained across three plays. The treatment of Falstaff and Hotspur reveals a growing interest in the potential of subsidiary characters' contributions to the total effect. Both plays contain sombre moments and touches of high comic relief. Both plays move with imagination and creativity along the appointed rails of actual history, without allowing the fact to appear a confinement or limitation. Serious political and social issues are punctuated by swift and spectacular action. Both plays, finally, centre upon the sense of "conflict" and bristle with tension—embodied, at their heart, in the seeming contradictory paradox of Hal himself.

Much of this dramatic tension and conflict has left the action by the time of *Henry V*. The play, however, remains a fitting culmination to the three-play cycle. In terms of Henry's character (now settled and firmly established), language and spectacle, the play is more of a patriotic celebration at the height of Elizabeth's reign. Issues and ideals at the centre of the action in the previous two plays are now satisfyingly resolved, justified and fulfilled.

Because of the essential nature of the plays, I have chosen to see *Julius Caesar, Antony and Cleopatra* and *Coriolanus* as Roman Histories rather than as conventional tragedies. Of these plays, only *Coriolanus* in any way follows the normal pattern of tragedy, or even the pattern of Shakespeare's tragedies. The focus in these three plays is much broader than a single concentration upon one man's downfall. *Julius Caesar* certainly offers powerfully drawn characters in conflict with one another (and in Brutus's case, in conflict with himself)—yet this is seen, in presentation, as a conflict of ideology. Certainly, we are deeply concerned with Brutus's sense of honour, Antony's opportunism, Cassius's sense

---

[5] Ironically, the very next history, *The Life and Death of King John*, is a curious, unsatisfactory play that is rarely performed.

79

of injustice and Casca's jealousy. We are also aware that these elements colour and shape the action. However, by removing the "main character" halfway through the play and by spreading character interest across a number of protagonists, we do not become immersed in one or two deeply engaging psychological portraits in the manner of the tragedies. As in Brecht's concept of epic theatre, we are able to distance ourselves from character and action and concentrate upon the play's "thought". Even allowing for the play's powerful elements of language and spectacle, it is this which tends to remain the play's abiding preoccupation.

Similarly, there is no neat "tragic pattern" to *Antony and Cleopatra*, though here the dramatist narrows the political issue and develops the psychological realism of the main characters. We are also deeply involved in the lovers' great struggle to overcome internal (Antony's sense of duty) and external (Octavius) forces that threaten to keep them apart. However, it is highly contentious as to whether the play's ending is "tragic" in the true sense. Throughout the play, their love is presented with a superhuman, other-worldly dimension. In death, they are "united"and Cleopatra's final words evoke such strong images of an after-life that we have a strong sense of their love continuing. As an audience, we are unable to forget the lengthening shadow of Octavius's inevitable success and the inexorable march of the Roman Empire through one of its more turbulent turmoils.

Coriolanus does follow the tragic format of a dominant, noble spirit brought low by inner weakness and external elements. Yet Coriolanus is deliberately presented in a manner that alienates and distances the audience's sympathy. This once more allows for concentration on the fascinating political events and philosophies. This is further enhanced by the series of largely undeveloped secondary characters (apart, of course, from the marvellous achievement of Volumnia—though even this character is more important for what she *represents* than what she actually *is*)—which, from a play written in 1608, by a dramatist at the peak of his dramatic powers, we can only assume to be a conscious device.

SHAKESPEARE AND THE LATE ROMANCES

Shakespeare's final four plays (discounting *Henry VIII*, which appears a colloboration) also require distinctive categorisation. They are again different from anything previously produced by the dramatist. Perhaps

Shakespeare was once more attempting to go beyond the confines of "pure" tragedy or comedy. More simply, the challenge of writing for a new type of theatre (indoors) may have resulted in the new type of Drama.

Pericles is a veritable Pandora's Box of dramatic elements. There are moments of tragic intensity, as the protagonist appears to "lose"both wife and daughter, yet the resolution is one of restored harmony and happiness. Character and action are developed in poetic and symbolic, rather than "realistic", terms. Spectacle—enhanced by constant "masque" elements of mime and music and lyrically atmospheric language—is more pronounced than in the previous plays. Cymbeline continues the development of such poetic, symbolic and pastoral Drama— though here the sense of evil is more sharply focused and potentially more dangerous. This symbolism of the Late Romances centres heavily upon the use of the young girl as a saviour figure. From such a seemingly fragile and helpless source emanates a beauty, truth and innocence that is now seen as capable of purifying evil and regenerating the positive elements of life. The child quite forcefully becomes "father" to the father and leads him on the path to wisdom and awareness. Such heroines in the Late Romances are a curious amalgamation of the audacious and vivacious heroines of the great comedies and the more passive heroines of the tragedies, such as Ophelia, Desdemona and Cordelia.

This theme achieves its most vivid presentation in the final two plays. Indeed, Pericles and Cymbeline, although of interest in their own right, are perhaps best seen as experimental preparations for the more satisfying and successful creations of The Winter's Tale and The Tempest. The Winter's Tale continues the use of pastoral, yet with a firmer sense of character and symbolic purpose. There is a surer balance of dramatic elements, especially in the potential tragedy of Leontes' jealousy against the pastoral idyll of the lovers and the comic invention of Autolycus. The language now strives for a form of poetic realism. In other words, the essence of the human condition is portrayed in the manner of poetry, indirectly suggested and implied through symbol and image. The raging jealousy of Leontes and his equally abrupt contrition are not designed to appear realistic or naturalistic, yet such behaviour appears entirely credible within the context of the world that the play creates. What we have now is the total effect of the poetic dramatic experience, where we are not ostensibly aware of particular elements, such as character, action or thought, but rather captivated by the entire unified poetic process. Like some dramatic concerto, we are moved by the whole piece, without consciously being aware of individual sections or instruments. We are held by the steady, mystical and poetic rhythm, in much the same way as Caliban is by the island's haunting music in the final play:

...the isle is full of noises,
Sounds, and sweet airs, that give delight and hurt not.
Sometimes a thousand twangling instruments
Will hum about mine ears; and sometimes voices,
That, if then I had waked after long sleep,
Will make me sleep again; and then, in dreaming,
The clouds methought, would open and show riches
Ready to drop upon me: that, when I waked,
I cried to dream again.

The Tempest itself is a remarkably satisfying finale to Shakespeare's dramatic career. It is tempting to read much into Prospero's situation—the master illusionist, at the height of his power, with the complete ability to charm or frighten through the host of devices at his disposal, finally relinquishing his book and staff, his "art", for quiet retirement. Whether or not Shakespeare was offering a dramatic presentation of his own situation is irrelevant to the success of this play as a work of art. The entire piece is beautifully structured. A closer than usual obedience to the Unities creates a concentrated intensity. The theme of love, especially in its broader, humanitarian dimensions, is held in detailed focus—together with the other issues of revenge, rulership and gratitude. The bestial Caliban promotes speculation on the perennial concept of the "noble savage". The language spins an exotic web of lyrical, poetic symbolism. The tension of the central conflict—will Prospero choose revenge or forgiveness?—rivets the attention throughout. The serious elements of the play are balanced by the broad humour of Stephano and the witty discontent of Trinculo. There are haunting interludes of masque-like mime and music. Yet above all this, we have Prospero himself, dwarfing all other elements of the play, a character of rich psychological realism and resonant symbolism, controlling events like some master puppeteer—before finally realising that it is not given to human beings to "play the god" and that all we can strive for is compassion, understanding and forgiveness.

CONCLUSION

The above survey, necessarily brief and generalised, concentrates on Shakespeare's development as a working, practising playwright. For above all else, this is what he was. In terms of plot, character and action, Shakespeare actually *creates* very little; not one background situation to any of the plays is an original. However, by concentrating on developing his facility for presenting the essential ingredients of Drama—plot, character, thought, language, conflict, climax, etc.—Shakespeare quite rapidly developed the ability to fashion unique and enduring dramatic creations from his well-worn sources.

FOR THE STUDENT

The student should now have some awareness of how his or her "set plays" on the Shakespeare Paper relate to the general body of Shakespeare's work as a whole. The student will also be able to see the other plays which relate specifically and directly to those set plays and should make every effort to become more familiar with them. As a general reading list for Shakespeare, I would suggest:

- *Romeo and Juliet*
- *The Merchant of Venice*
- *As You Like It*
- *Hamlet*
- *Henry IV, Part 1*
- *Othello*
- *The Tempest*

CHAPTER 11

DRAMA AND THE EXAMINATION

In the previous chapters we have looked in some detail at the various background elements of Drama in general. This is a crucial part of any A-Level course in English Literature, as the stated aim of all the examining boards is to "encourage an enjoyment and appreciation of English Literature based on an *informed* personal response and to extend this appreciation where it has already been acquired". The material used in these chapters provides that "informed" basis which the student may now apply, as relevant, to the specific items of Drama on the chosen syllabus.

We have already noted that Drama extends across *all* the examination papers that are likely to confront the student. However, the different requirements of these papers will mean that the factors and elements we have been discussing need to be tailored and slanted differently for each paper. We may now look specifically at Drama in this examination context and explore how the background material is to be adapted and developed for particular purposes.

DRAMA AND THE UNSEEN PASSAGES PAPER

The student may well be faced with an extract from a play with which he or she will, most likely, be totally unfamiliar. The intention of such an exercise will be to test the student's ability to approach Drama "critically". This "unknown quantity" element to the Comment and Appreciation Paper often strikes terror into the hearts of students preparing for the examination. What if I get a poem, or a passage from a novel, or an extract from a play, that I cannot begin to understand? This is the perennial lament and fear of students in their final months of preparation.

The task, however, is nowhere near as daunting or impossible as it may at first appear. The paper requires *comment* and *appreciation*, not some profound thesis on essential meaning, either of the passage, or the work it comes from. The examiners are only too aware of the limited scope offered in the discussion of extracts as opposed to entire works. What the examiner *does* expect from the student is an awareness of the elements and techniques that are basic to the literary medium in question—poetry, prose, Drama—and some assessment of how these are individually and particularly employed and developed in a given example. It is not a test of comprehension—although this will inevitably become part of the process. It is more an assessment of the student's ability to apply an *informed* awareness of the conventions of, in this case, Drama in an appreciation of the given working sample.

Comforted by their "safe" body of knowledge and theme, character, imagery, etc. when it comes to "set plays", students sometimes feel a little lost, bereft of known landmarks, when they face "unseen" passages. How can we possibly prepare for such passages when we have no idea where they may come from, or what they may mean? This again is to miss the particular point of this paper. Such landmarks are still there and have to be equally well known and successfully applied; it is simply a question of different emphasis.

In terms of this specific examination and the material we have already discussed, the student will primarily be concerned here with the *elements* of Drama. He or she will need a firm grounding in the basics of how *plot* is developed and paced; how *character* is created and expanded; how *conflict* is employed for dramatic tension; how *exposition*, *complication*, *climax* and *resolution* are presented; how *theme* and *thought* are integrated into the action; how *language* may be used to create character, mood, tone, or atmosphere; how the technicalities of *aside*, *soliloquy*,*music*, *spectacle*, etc. may be employed to create and enhance a particular effect; and so on. In other words, this paper will require the student to be fully conversant with the sort of details we examined in chapters 4-8 and to have sufficiently digested and assimilated their importance, through frequent practice, so as to be able to apply their significance to the given examination extract.

This would satisfy the *basic* requirement of any such examination. However, if a student is thoroughly versed in *all* the background material we have looked at, he or she will then be able to provide the *developed* and advanced response by offering relevant and perceptive observations concerning the ways in which the given extract might relate to the nature, essence, forms and tradition of Drama as well. It is in these areas that the outstanding and committed candidate will begin to shine and excel, by revealing the ways in which he or she has been able to develop and expand the basic informed response.

Not all the elements of Drama will be equally relevant to any one given passage. Indeed, the way in which the student is able to select and highlight those which *are* is a further test of the candidate's perceptive handling of the medium (what the examiners term the student's *sensibility*). In view of this, there are certain important considerations the student should keep in mind long before the actual examination.

Firstly,the extracts chosen will not be random scenes from random plays. They will be *significant* or *key scenes* taken from major pieces of Drama. The most common types of significant scene (and the sort of implications and considerations they will involve) are as follows:

Opening scenes

These provide a favourite source of "extract" material. There is an obvious reason for this; the reader is not suddenly dropped into the middle of the action. The play confronts the student in the same initial way it would any reader or audience and nothing has been "missed" as it were.

What the student will be mainly concerned with in such a scene are the techniques employed by the dramatist to arouse immediate audience interest. There will be something of interest, perhaps even unusual, about the characters, or their interaction, or the background situation. The style of the language will immediately establish a *tone* or *atmosphere* for this crucial early stage of the play.

The student will need to pay particular attention here to the element of *exposition*. In other words, is the necessary background information about character and situation, which will lay the essential foundation for the ensuing action, given with economy and clarity?

The basic question the student must ask about such a scene is quite simple: what is there in this opening extract that stimulates our interest to want to know more about what is going to happen?

Character scenes

These would be scenes specifically concerned with developing our perception of the character, or characters, involved. We have already looked in some detail at the techniques of dramatic characterisation and this information will need to be fully assimilated and applied perceptively if such an extract is to be successfully tackled. Again, the student should pay special attention to the ways in which language is used to shade the character of a speaker, or the person he might be talking about.

Complication scenes

These are the sort of scenes where the plot (to use an old dramatic cliché) "thickens". They are important interludes that will turn and direct all the play's future action. The student will need to call upon the full range of dramatic "elements", as relevant, to highlight the manner in which the given scene develops its complexity and sense of intrigue.

Atmosphere scenes

These are the sort of scenes that will largely promote the distinctive, perhaps unique, atmosphere achieved by certain plays (*Midsummer Night's Dream, Macbeth, King Lear, Waiting for Godot* being the more obvious type of examples). The main concern here will be in the use of *dramatic language*. Elements of "spectacle"—mime, music, dance, etc.—may also be employed in such passages.

There are other types of scene that may also be offered for consideration. These might include scenes in which a *crisis* or *climax* in the action is reached, where the focus will centre upon *stagecraft*—i.e. how the characters are "arranged" about the stage, entrance and exit, how dialogue and language are used to promote the sense of crisis or climax. (Such scenes are less likely to be offered, however, as they essentially depend so much on what has gone before and tend to be somewhat unsatisfactory in "extracted" form.) Scenes containing a high emotional content—love, hate, rivalry, tragic loss—also lend themselves to this particular examination format. The initial emphasis here will again be with character and language, as it will with scenes attempting to promote humour.

CONCLUSION

When faced with the "unseen" extract exercise, the student must begin by asking one basic question: what is the main purpose and aim of the given passage? If the implications of this question are deeply and relevantly considered, they will lend naturally to the particular dramatic elements that are of prime importance in the passage. Having done this, there remains one further, preparatory consideration before the successful analysis may begin. This concerns the *general* and the *particular*. The student should consider what general elements of dramatic technique the passage reveals (in common with most other plays) and then what *specific* elements of technique, style, presentation, etc. are present to give this extract its *individual*, perhaps unique, distinctiveness. In other words, the student must realise the examiner is looking for evidence of the candidate's ability in two areas: (a) a basic knowledge and awareness of dramatic technique that enables the student to offer relevant observations of a general nature on any given example of Drama, and (b) how that basic awareness has been developed by the student to promote specific and perceptive observations that distinguish and discriminate the given example in relation to all other plays. The "average" script will frequently do no more than (a), while the outstanding script will develop (a) into (b).

One final consideration remains and this is the question of *dialogue*. Given the type of medium Drama is, dialogue is quite obviously its lifeblood. Because of this, it is more than just the use of language (though that is obviously an important, even crucial element). It relates, in its wider implications, into all areas of plot, character, thought and so on. When considering dialogue, a series of questions should again form in the student's mind. Is the dialogue convincing as speech?—i.e. does it "sound" like people in conversation or people making speeches at one another? Is each speaker's dialogue sufficiently distinguished and different to provide a sense of individual characterisation? How does the dialogue affect the pace, movement and rhythm of the action? Once such *general* aspects have been considered, the student may again develop this into observations on the *specific*, individual use of dialogue in the passage before him.

DRAMA AND THE SHAKESPEARE PAPER

In terms of this examination and, for that matter, any other set plays on other examination papers, the student should be aware of what "skills" the examiner is "testing". These may be itemised as:

1. **Knowledge** – of the content of the play and where appropriate of the personal and historical circumstances in which it was written;

2. **Understanding** – extending from factual comprehension to a wider concept of the nature and significance of the play;

3. **Analysis** – the ability to recognise and describe dramatic technique and the use of language;

4. **Judgment** – the capacity to make judgments of value based on close reading;

5. **Sense of the Past and Tradition** – the ability to see a play in its historical literary context as well as that of the present day;

6. **Expression** – the ability to write organised and cogent essays on the given material.

On the Shakespeare Paper, the method of assessing these "skills" is two-fold. As these two elements are tested separately, and as they require a different approach, we will look at them individually.

(a) **The Context Question**

For this section of the examination, the syllabus stipulates that questions requiring "explanation, comment and appreciation" concerning specific passages from the set plays will be asked. The passages concerned will be quoted in full on the Paper itself. Such an exercise is specifically designed to assess "skills" 1, 3 and 4 outlined above. They are basically seeking evidence as to the depth and detail of knowledge a student possesses about the play and the awareness of the play's particular characteristics.

Context questions usually provide three sections that follow the criteria outlined above. The first section will deal with *explanation*. The student will be expected to "explain" the passage in terms of its actual meaning and what is happening. The second section will involve *comment* as to why this particular passage, in itself, is significant and how it relates to the play as a whole. The extract is likely to be the sort of "key scene" we have already noted and will be significant for developing character, plot, or theme. The exercise initially tests the candidate's *depth* of knowledge of the play, by asking for the passage to be "located" and explained and then moves on to the breadth of awareness by asking for the significance of the passage in relation to the play as a whole.

The most demanding element of the context question requires *appreciation*. This will test the student's awareness of the play's characteristic technique and use of language from a given sample. Observations here will be similar to those made on "unseen" passages and will look at the specific way the given set play makes its own individual use of the elements of Drama such as characterisation, development of plot and, primarily, use of language.

(b) **The Essay Question**

In the essay section, the student will encounter "general questions on the significance, subject-matter and dramatic qualities of the plays prescribed". It is here that the student will have to display a *detailed* awareness of the play's characteristic elements of characterisation, theme, use of language and dramatic technique. The candidate should also endeavour, at all times, to support observations with direct reference, detail and example (ideally quotation) from the play itself. To say, for instance, that Macbeth agonises over killing the king is not enough; we should also be told where and when, and in what terms.

Relevant observations may also be made in such questions to the ways in which the play relates to the general tradition of Drama, or the dramatist's own other plays. The whole exercise, in fact, allows the student to show just how far a basic understanding of the play has been achieved and to what extent this has been developed.

DRAMA AND THE SET PLAY

Most of the observations made above on the Shakespeare Paper apply equally to other set plays. Some boards offer context questions on this Paper as well—where the aims and criteria and implications outlined above are exactly the same. The essay questions will also, in the same way, range across the full spectrum of dramatic elements and allow the student to display to what degree of sophistication and complexity the basic understanding of the play has been developed.

CHAPTER 12

THE WRITTEN ANALYSIS

The previous chapter looked at the general format taken by Drama in the examination. We may now look at this process *in practice*, through a series of working examples. As in the previous books on Poetry and Prose, these sample analyses are not intended as model answers. They are designed to indicate the way in which such questions may be approached and show the sort of depth and detail a student could be reasonably expected to achieve in the time allowed. The samples will by no means say everything that could be said about the particular passages, but will hopefully present a structured example of the type and range of comment expected in a developed answer.

1. THE UNSEEN EXTRACT

It is worth remembering exactly what it is that the syllabus for this examination stipulates: that "the intention of the questions is to test the candidate's ability to read literature critically"; that the student will be required to "organise his response to unseen passages"; and that the student should be able to "present that response as clearly and directly as possible". This emphasises the basic process: a careful and sensitive reading, the organisation of the ideas that arise from that reading, and the presentation of those ideas in a coherent written analysis.

Examination instructions also require candidates to "read carefully" and "refer directly" to the passage. Observations made should always be supported by reference to, or quotation from, the passage itself. Indeed, the student should take full advantage of the fact that the text in question is given. Unlike essay questions, quotations, as such, do not have to be learned by heart. On this paper, quotation may be used much more liberally as evidence for points made. Lengthy quotations, however, should be avoided; here, a general line or section reference will suffice.

The actual analysis will usually be structured around a series of specific questions that the examiner will employ to direct candidates to the crucial aspects of the extract. Needless to say, these questions must be *read carefully* and *considered* in some depth for an awareness of their *full* implications and requirements.

The following represents a typical dramatic extract accompanied by the type of questions to be found in such an exercise. The sample analysis will be found directly after the questions.

Q. The following extract is taken from the opening of a play. Read the passage carefully then answer the questions that follow.

[LADY SNEERWELL *discovered at her toilet*; SNAKE *drinking chocolate.*]

LADY SNEERWELL: The paragraphs, you say, Mr Snake, were all inserted?

SNAKE: They were, madam; and, as I copied them myself in a feigned hand, there can be no suspicion whence they came.

LADY SNEERWELL: Did you circulate the report of Lady Brittle's intrigue with Captain Boastall?

SNAKE: That's in as fine a train as your ladyship could wish. In the common course of things, I think it must reach Mrs Clackitt's ears within four-and-twenty hours; and then, you know, the business is as good as done.

LADY SNEERWELL: Why, truly, Mrs Clackitt has a very pretty talent, and a great deal of industry.

SNAKE: True, madam, and has been tolerably successful in her day. To my knowledge, she has been the cause of six matches being broken off, and three sons being disinherited; of four forced elopements, nine separate maintenances, and two divorces. Nay, I have more than once traced her causing a "tete a tete" in the "Town and Country Magazine", when the parties, perhaps, had never seen each other's faces before in the course of their lives.

LADY SNEERWELL: She certainly has talents, but her manner is gross.

SNAKE: "Tis very true. She generally designs well, has a free tongue and a bold invention; but her colouring is too dark, and her outlines often extravagant.She wants that delicacy of tint, and mellowness of sneer, which distinguishes your ladyship's scandal.

LADY SNEERWELL: You are partial, Snake.

SNAKE: Not in the least; everybody allows that Lady Sneerwell can do more with a word or look than many can with the most laboured detail, even when they happen to have a little truth on their side to support it.

LADY SNEERWELL: Yes, my dear Snake; and I am no hypocrite to deny the satisfaction I reap from the success of my efforts. Wounded myself, in the early part of my life, by the envenomed tongue of slander, I confess I have since known no pleasure equal to reducing others to the level of my own reputation.

SNAKE: Nothing could be more natural. But, Lady Sneerwell, there is one affair in which you have lately employed me, wherein, I confess, I am at a loss to guess your motives.

LADY SNEERWELL: I conceive you mean with respect to my neighbour, Sir Peter Teazle, and his family?

SNAKE: I do. Here are two young men, to whom Sir Peter has acted as a kind of guardian since their father's death; the eldest possessing the most amiable character, and universally well spoken of—the youngest, the most dissipated and extravagant young fellow in the kingdom, without friends or character: the former an avowed admirer of your ladyship, and apparently your favourite; the latter attached to

93

Maria, Sir Peter's ward, and confessedly beloved by her. Now, on the face of these circumstances, it is utterly unaccountable to me, why you, the widow of a city knight, with a good jointure, should not close with the passion of a man of such character and expectations as Mr Surface; and more so why you should be so uncommonly earnest to destroy the mutual attachment subsisting between his brother Charles and Maria.

LADY SNEERWELL: Then, at once to unravel this mystery, I must inform you that love has no share whatever in the intercourse between Mr Surface and me.

SNAKE: No!

LADY SNEERWELL: His real attachment is to Maria, or her fortune; but, finding in his brother a favoured rival, he has been obliged to mask his pretensions, and profit by my assistance.

SNAKE: Yet still I am more puzzled why you should interest yourself in his success.

LADY SNEERWELL: Heavens! how dull you are! Cannot you surmise the weakness which I hitherto, through shame, have concealed even from you? Must I confess that Charles—that extravagant, that bankrupt in fortune and reputation—that he it is for whom I am thus anxious and malicious, and to gain whom I would sacrifice everything?

SNAKE: Now, indeed your conduct appears consistent: but how came you and Mr Surface so confidential?

LADY SNEERWELL: For our mutual interest. I have found him out a long time since. I know him to be artful, selfish, and malicious—in short, a sentimental knave; while with Sir Peter, and indeed with all his acquaintances, he passes for a youthful miracle of prudence, good sense, and benevolence.

SNAKE: Yes, yet Sir Peter vows he has not his equal in England; and, above all, he praises him as a man of sentiment.

LADY SNEERWELL: True; and with the assistance of his sentiment and hypocrisy he has brought Sir Peter entirely into his interest with regard to Maria; while poor Charles has no friend in the house— though, I fear, he has a powerful one in Maria's heart, against whom we must direct our schemes.

(a) Summarise briefly the situation that is being presented in this extract. (10 marks)
(b) How effective do you find this extract as the opening of a play? What is there to promote our interest in what is to come? (40 marks)

(a) This extract centres exclusively on a conversation between Lady Sneerwell and her apparent "confidant", Snake. They begin by discussing a piece of business that has already taken place—the circulation of a letter reporting the "intrigue" of one Lady Brittle and a Captain Boastall. To ensure this seemingly scandalous gossip achieves a wide audience, Snake has passed the news in the direction of one Mrs Clackitt. Mrs Clackitt's great talent for spreading destructive scandal is testified to at some length, though Snake proclaims Mrs Clackitt's "talent" lacks the distinctive, superior style of Lady Sneerwell herself.

We are then introduced to what will presumably be the main action of the play. This comes with Snake's confusion as to Lady Sneerwell's motives and interest concerning the family of her neighbour, Sir Peter Teazle. We learn of two guardians, both young men, the one apparently a paragon of civilised virtue, the other, his brother, "the most dissipated and extravagant young fellow in the kingdom". Sir Peter also has a young ward, Maria, who loves, and is loved by, the dissolute brother Charles Surface. Lady Sneerwell, apparently herself an eligible widow, appears most affectionate towards the other brother, known here simply as Mr Surface. Snake is therefore at a loss to understand why Lady Sneerwell should be employing her considerable talents to destroy the relationship between Charles and Maria, as there seems to be no possible benefit in this for Lady Sneerwell.

Lady Sneerwell clarifies the mystery. Mr Surface is anything but the paragon he appears; he is, in fact, scheming and deceitful. He also wants Maria (or her fortune) for himself and has joined forces with Lady Sneerwell, who now confesses her own desire for Charles, to destroy the present relationship between Charles and Maria, to his own (and Lady Sneerwell's) advantage.

(b) The extract provides a most successful opening scene by immediately establishing intriguing and unusual situations and characters and by quickly achieving and developing a distinctive style, tone and humour.

Audience interest is basically stimulated by three factors: situation, character and use of language. In terms of situation, we are instantly in the middle of unusual and (literally) intriguing circumstances. We are presented with a group of people (the two speakers and their named associates) who discuss scandal, malicious gossip and destructive rumour as if it were a science, or some advanced art form:

> her colouring is too dark, and her outlines often extravagant. She wants that delicacy of tint, and mellowness of sneer, which distinguish your ladyships's scandal.

After the humorous list of Mrs Clackitt's "achievements", we move on to the intriguing complexities of the main plot situation. In this, we find Lady Sneerwell seemingly attracted to Mr Surface, yet secretly setting her sights upon his brother, Charles; Mr Surface himself, far from what he appears, has designs upon Maria, who is already in love with Charles; and the dangerous alliance between Lady Sneerwell and Mr Surface, determined to upset the blossoming relationship between Charles and Maria to their own mutual advantage. With skilful economy and clarity, the situation is speedily offered and developed and the audience are already eager to see how its complexities will unravel.

Our interest is also aroused by the characters, both those we see on the stage and those we hear about and will meet later. Here we have a play in which the characters are instantly "characterised" by their names—Sneerwell, Snake, Clackitt, Brittle, Boastall, Surface. Such a device may not appear very subtle or sophisticated as a means of characterisation, yet in what we already sense will be some form of satire on the pretensions and hypocrisy of the fashionable and wealthy "idle" privileged classes, it proves a sharp and effective touch. One of the finest English dramatic satirists, Ben Jonson, regularly employed just such a device.

From the outset, the characters live up to their names. Lady Sneerwell displays a sense of aristocratic superiority in relation to the likes of Mrs Clackitt and even Snake. Lavish testimony is offered concerning her talent for scandal-mongering. Further interest is added by her revelation of her reasons for embarking on such an unusual "career":

> Wounded myself, in the early part of my life, by the envenomed

tongue of slander, I confess I have since known no pleasure equal to reducing others to the level of my own reputation.

From this opening scene, we do not suspect that this will be a play to offer profound psychological insight, yet this adds an intriguing dimension to Lady Sneerwell's character. This is further developed by her observations concerning the two brothers. Her scheming manipulation of this situation reveals a calculating, selfish opportunism, yet she also talks of her love for Charles—"to gain whom I would sacrifice everything".

The role of the splendidly-named Snake is less complex. In this scene, it is essentially a dramatic device to "shade" the character of Lady Sneerwell and to act as the confidant to whom the intrigue of plot concerning Sir Peter Teazle's family may be revealed. In himself, he appears little more than obsequious flatterer and lackey. He is no doubt essential to Lady Sneerwell's schemes (as we see from the way he has arranged the matter of Lady Brittle and Captain Boastall at the beginning), yet, for all his deferential reverence towards Lady Sneerwell, we sense that even she is somewhat contemptuous of Snake ("Heavens! how dull you are!").

We also find effective use here of characterisation by report. Even before we see them on stage, audience interest is aroused in the Surface brothers. The elder Mr Surface has achieved a widespread reputation for being the "most amiable character, and universally well spoken of", "a youthful miracle of prudence, good sense, and benevolence". However, true to his name, Lady Sneerwell has found him out as "artful, selfish, malicious". Such successful masters of deceit and pretense, such artful dissemblers, have always fascinated audiences—we need look no further than Iago, Edmund, or even Hal—and we are eager to meet this one. We also anticipate the workings of the devious alliance with Lady Sneerwell. Similarly, we are intrigued by the younger brother, Charles, "the most dissipated and extravagant young fellow in the kingdom"—though we might already suspect, from the situation regarding his brother and the fact that he is loved by Maria, that he is also undeserving of his reputation.

Added to this powerful recipe for character interaction, we have the controlling guardian figure of Sir Peter Teazle, who appears to accept the "surface" characters of the two brothers and miss the reality. In this way, a short opening scene has developed a rich potential for complex and comic character relationships enmeshed in a plot of intrigue and attempted manipulation.

The language used in the extract establishes a refined, sophisticated tone in keeping with the aristocratic setting. For the modern audience, the phrasing has an almost quaint formality:

> I must inform you that love has no share whatever in the intercourse between Mr Surface and me.

This leads to the sophisticated humour of the passage, which derives largely from such "elevated" characters employing refined, elaborate expression to a subject as petty as scandal-mongering, as in Snake's:

> She wants the delicacy of tint, and mellowness of sneer, which distinguish your ladyship's scandal.

Humour also arises from the way in which language is employed as part of the scene's general inversion of all decent, respectable values. With a serious precision that heightens the humour, Snake itemises Mrs Clackitt's "achievements":

> To my knowledge, she has been the cause of six matches being broken off, and three sons being disinherited; of four forced elopements, nine separate maintenances and two divorces.

Lady Sneerwell greets Snake's testimony of her own powers of promoting scandal, described in appreciative, artistic tones, with a flattered, mock-modest "You are partial, Snake". This comically gross inversion of values is perhaps best captured in Snake's avowal that Lady Sneerwell can "do more with a word or look than many can with the most laboured detail, even when they happen to have a little truth on their side to support it". The almost irrelevant, casual reference to "little truth" provides a marvellous effect of comic understatement.

These, then, are the elements in the extract that promote audience interest. Taken together, the complex plot, intriguing, yet morally dubious characters and refined language, with its sophisticated, at times outrageous wit, strongly suggest the opening of a skilfully constructed Restoration Comedy.

CONCLUSION

We can see from the above how the typical Drama Unseen Passage question works. The passage itself is from a play's opening (in this case, Sheridan's *The School for Scandal*), as this offers most scope for authentic analysis. The opening question, which, it will be noted, carried far less marks, is designed to assess the candidate's basic comprehension of the passage. The answer will indicate if a student has misread or misunderstood the passage and therefore enables the examiner to make allowances, where necessary or possible, in the second question. This second question is the crucial element and tests a candidate's awareness of the various components of Drama as they relate to the given example.

2. THE CONTEXT QUESTION

In this exercise, the examiners will offer an extract from a play which the student has already studied in detail. This is usually the case on the Shakespeare Paper and with other pieces of Drama studied on the other papers. Although certain observations on dramatic technique here may overlap with the Unseen Passage Paper, it is basically a different exercise. The candidate is expected to display *detailed* awareness of a specific text based on a characteristic and significant extract. Here is a working example:

> **Q.** Read the following extract from *Othello* carefully and then answer the questions below.

IAGO: Thus do I ever make my fool my purse;
        For I mine own gain'd knowledge should profane
        If I would time expend with such a snipe
        But for my sport and profit. I hate the Moor;
        And it is thought abroad that "twixt my sheets
        He has done my office: I know not if't be true;
        But I, for mere suspicion in that kind,
        Will do as if for surety. He holds me well;
        The better shall my purpose work on him.
        Cassio's a proper man: let me see now;
        To get his place, and to plume up my will
        In double knavery,—How, how?—Let's see:—
        After sometime to abuse Othello's ear
        That he is too familiar with his wife:—
        He hath a person, and a smooth dispose,
        To be suspected; fram'd to make women false.

The Moor is of a free and open nature,
That thinks men honest that but seem to be so;
And will as tenderly be led by the nose
As asses are.
I have't;—it is engender'd:—hell and night
Must bring this monstrous birth to the world's light.

(a) What is the context and significance of this extract?
(b) What is revealed here of the speaker's character?
(c) Comment on the use of dramatic language in this extract.

(a) This extract presents Iago's soliloquy at the close of Act I. In one respect, it is the most significant moment in the play, as Iago here begins to conceive the nature and scope of his "revenge". The main early business of the play has, it appears, been happily concluded. Othello has married Desdemona in secret, defended himself success-fully against the dangerous charges made by her father, Brabantio, and been given the illustrious appointment of commander-in-chief in the war against the Turks. His commission at Cyprus (and Desdemona's presence there) has been arranged and Cassio is to stand as his lieuten-ant. In this extract, we find the only, yet vital, "loose end": Iago's sense of grievance.

Just prior to the soliloquy, Iago has enlisted the assistance of the disappointed and love-sick Roderigo—the "snipe" to whom he so contemptuously refers. In the extract itself, Iago slowly unravels the web that will satisfy his hatred and desire for revenge on Othello (for not making Iago his lieutenant after years of faithful service and on the suspicion that Othello has had an affair with Emilia, Iago's wife) and Cassio (for taking what Iago assumes to be his own rightful appoint-ment and out of jealousy for his handsome good looks and charm). Iago here hits upon the notion of implicating Othello's wife Desdemona in an "affair" with Cassio. This is the embryonic "double knavery" that will now direct the ensuing action of the entire play.

(b) This speech provides important insights into Iago's character. In the previous action, we have already seen Iago "playing his parts"— devoted friend (to Roderigo), concerned citizen (to Brabantio) and faith-ful servant (to Othello). Now, through the dramatic solioquy, we see Iago as he really is for the first time.

The first thing we sense is Iago's arrogance, amounting, in effect, to some sort of "superiority complex". Roderigo, on whose behalf he has been so earnestly solicitous in the previous speeches, is dismissed as a "snipe", one on whom Iago feels he would be "profaning" his "own gain'd knowledge" were there not "sport" and "profit" in the association. He then moves on to consider his attitude to Othello, where his observation is dramatically blunt: "I hate the Moor". He then begins to engage in what Coleridge termed his "motive-hunting"—as if he feels he needs to justify this all-consuming hatred with valid reasons. There is a suspicion of adultery between Othello and Iago's wife Emilia. Iago acknowledges there is no evidence, yet the mere suspicion, as far as he is concerned, will "do as if for surety".

The next consideration is Iago's own position in relation to Othello. He realises Othello holds him in great trust and resolves, in the coldest, most calculating manner, to use this to his advantage. In contemplating how to supplant Cassio, Iago reveals another important dimension to his character. The intention is not simply to achieve Cassio's place, but also to "plume up my will". Iago wants the satisfaction to his monstrous ego of impressing his "superiority" on others by being able to manipulate events to his advantage.

Ironically, however, there is some justification for this sense of superiority within the next few lines. With inventive speed of mind and a sharp, perceptive grasp of human nature (especially Othello's "free and open nature" and Cassio's "smooth dispose"), Iago manages to formulate his plan for revenge in an impressively short space of time. Yet we are not allowed to "admire" Iago for long. In the final lines, we see the gloating, vindictive contempt for Othello:

That thinks men honest that but seem to be so;
And will as tenderly be led by the nose
As asses are...

and the destructive, malignant determination to achieve the "monstrous birth" of his revenge.

(c) The language of this extract is designed mainly to "colour" the character of the speaker. We have just had an act dominated by the grand eloquence of Othello, the Duke, Brabantio and Desdemona. The act now ends on the low-key, yet contrastingly effective and ominous, down-to-earth bluntness of Iago. After Othello has delivered his considerably "varnish'd" speech, we now find plain, forceful language ("snipe", "hate", "led by the nose") and bold, direct statement ("Thus do I ever make my fool my purse", "I hate the Moor").

In dramatic terms, however, the language also works at a more subtle level. The extract is in the form of a soliloquy and is supposed to give us the thoughts of the character "out loud". For this reason, we find Shakespeare attempting, through use of punctuation and language, a "realistic" presentation of the thought process in action, even though the soliloquy is in verse. We find this most effectively in the simple, contemplative phrases, such as: "He holds me well", "let me see now" and "How, how?" Here it is the very simplicity of language that convinces; we do not think in fanciful, elaborate terms, especially when formulating a plan of action; we seek clarity and perspective and direction, rather than trying to impress or convince with our expression.

The language of Iago's obsessive and vindictive passion for revenge has its own compelling power. This can be sensed in expressions such as:

> ...plume up my will
> in double knavery...

and:

> He hath a person, and a smooth dispose,
> To be suspected: fram'd to make women false.

It is, perhaps, seen at its finest in the dire, yet resounding couplet, with its marvellously controlled rhythm, that rounds off the entire act:

> I have't;—it is engender'd:—hell and night
> Must bring this monstrous birth to the world's light.

3. THE ESSAY QUESTION

There is little point in offering a sample answer when it comes to the essay question. As there are many approaches and angles possible in any given topic and as there are many ways of writing a good essay, it would be misleading to present something that might be considered a model answer. Instead, it might be more useful to suggest the sort of elements that generally contribute to a good essay answer.

There are certain preparations that should be undertaken *before* a student even attempts an essay answer. The student must ensure:

(a) that he or she has a firm grasp of the details of the actual play itself; there is a tendency to revise and concentrate upon the play's themes, implications, etc.—extraneous matter drawn *from* the play, yet not explicitly contained within it. The text itself must be known as thoroughly as possible; this includes a wide variety of direct, significant quotations.

(b) that once (a) has been assured, *then* the student may develop and strengthen an awareness of the work's themes and issues and the use it makes of the various dramatic elements;

(c) that he or she is aware of what such a question entails in the examination context; that if 40, or 45, minutes are allocated for that question, then that amount of time (and no more and certainly no less) is all that is required to provide a successful answer. This strict allocation of one's mental resources during the examination is a crucial, yet much neglected, factor in achieving success *across* the paper as a whole. It is never worth embellishing an essay on which the candidate feels "strong" to the detriment (in terms of time left available) of other questions.

When it comes to confronting actual essay questions, students should ensure that:

(i) they read the question carefully, considering the full implications and scope of the question and analysing just exactly what it is that is being required;

(ii) they arrange the material and quotation they feel will be relevant to the stated topic and plan its structuring to flow in a cogent, fluent and positive manner towards a well-argued conclusion;

(iii) they attempt, at all times, to support significant observations by means of direct quotation or detailed reference to the text;

(iv) they give due consideration and care to the expression and presentation of their answer.

CHAPTER 13

EXERCISES

The following is a series of full-length exercises. The intention is to provide as much practice as possible in all the varieties of Drama in the Advanced Level examination. With this in mind, Section A will offer extracts for the sort of directed comment required on the Unseen Passages Paper; Section B will provide extracts from Shakespeare and seeks to combine the "unseen" and the context exercise; Section C will offer generalised essay questions for Shakespeare and the works of other dramatists. These questions are necessarily generalised because the prescribed plays change from year to year, but the student will have no difficulty in applying them to the actual plays he or she may be studying.

SECTION A

1. Read the extract carefully then answer the questions that follow.

> [BLUNTSCHLI *has just inherited all his father's hotels and has asked for the hands of* RAINA, *daughter of* PETKOFF *and* CATHERINE, *in spite of her engagement to* SERGIUS SARANOFF.]

CATHERINE [*loftily polite*]: I doubt, sir, whether you quite realise either my daughter's position or that of Major Sergius Saranoff, whose place you propose to take. The Petkoffs and the Saranoffs are known as the richest and most important families in the country. Our position is almost historical: we can go back for twenty years.

PETKOFF: Oh never mind that Catherine. [*To Bluntschli*] We should be most happy, Bluntschli, if it were only a question of your position; but, hang it, you know Raina is accustomed to a very comfortable establishment. Sergius keep twenty horses.

BLUNTSCHLI: But who wants twenty horses? We're not going to keep a circus.

CATHERINE [*severely*]: My daughter, sir, is accustomed to a first-rate stable.

RAINA: Hush, mother: you're making me ridiculous.

BLUNTSCHLI: Oh well, if it comes to a question of an establishment, here goes! [*He darts impetuously to the table; seizes the papers in the blue envelope; and turns to Sergius.*] How many horses did you say?

SERGIUS: Twenty, noble Switzer.

BLUNTSCHLI: I have two hundred horses. [*They are amazed.*] How many carriages?

SERGIUS: Three.

BLUNTSCHLI: I have seventy. Twenty-four of them will hold twelve inside, besides two on the box, without counting the driver and conductor. How many tableclothes have you?

SERGIUS: How the deuce do I know?

BLUNTSCHLI: Have you four thousand?

SERGIUS: No.

BLUNTSCHLI: I have. I have nine thousand six hundred pairs of sheets and blankets, with two thousand four hundred eider-down quilts.I have ten thousand knives and forks, and the same quantity of dessert spoons. I have three hundred servants. I have six palatial establishments, besides two livery stables, a tea garden, and a private house. I have four medals for distinguished services; I have the rank of an officer and the standing of a gentleman; and I have three native languages. Show me any man in Bulgaria that can offer as much!

PETKOFF [*with childish awe*]: Are you the Emperor of Switzerland?

BLUNTSCHLI: My rank is the highest known in Switzerland: I am a free citizen.

CATHERINE: Then, Captain Bluntschli, since you are my daughter's choice—

RAINA [*mutinously*]: He's not.

CATHERINE [*ignoring her*]:—I shall not stand in the way of her happiness. [*Petkoff is about to speak.*] That is Major Petkoff's feeling also..

PETKOFF: Oh, I shall be only too glad. Two hundred horses! Whew!

SERGIUS: What says the lady?

RAINA [*pretending to sulk*]: The lady says that he can keep his table-clothes and his omnibuses. I am not here to be sold to the highest bidder. [*She turns her back on him.*]

BLUNTSCHLI: I won't take that answer. I appealed to you as a fugitive, a beggar, and a starving man. You accepted me. You gave me your hand to kiss, your bed to sleep in, and your roof to shelter me.

RAINA: I did not give them to the Emperor of Switzerland.

BLUNTSCHLI: That's just what I say. [*He catches her by the shoulder and turns her face-to-face with him.*] Now tell us whom you did give them to.

RAINA [*succumbing with a shy smile*]: To my chocolate cream soldier.

BLUNTSCHLI [*with a boyish laugh of delight*]: That'll do. Thank you.

(a) What impression do you form of the various characters in this extract?
(b) Examine the means employed here by the dramatist to create humour in this extract.

2. Read the extract carefully then answer the questions that follow.

[*By means of forbidden magic,* FAUSTUS *has summoned up the devil* MEPHISTOPHILIS *from hell.*]

MEPHIST: Now, Faustus, what wouldst thou have me do?

FAUST: I charge thee wait upon me whilst I live,
To do whatever Fastus shall command,

	Be it to make the moon drop from her sphere,
	Or the ocean to overwhelm the world.
MEPHIST:	I am a servant to great Lucifer,
	And may not follow thee without his leave:
	No more than he commands must we perform.
FAUST:	Did he not charge thee to appear to me?
MEPHIST:	No, I came hither of mine own accord.
FAUST:	Did not my conjuring speeches raise thee? speak.
MEPHIST:	That was the cause, but yet per accidens.[1]
	For, when we hear one rack the name of God,
	Abjure the Scriptures and his Saviour Christ,
	We fly, in hope, to get his glorious soul;
	Nor will we come, unless he use such means
	Whereby he is in danger to be damn'd.
	Therefore the shortest cut for conjuring
	Is stoutly to abjure the Trinity,
	And pray devoutly to the prince of hell.
FAUST:	So Faustus hath
	Already done; and holds this principle,
	There is no chief but only Belzebub;[2]
	To whom Faustus doth dedicate himself.
	This word "damnation" terrifies not him,
	For he confounds hell in Elysium:[3]
	His ghost be with the old philosophers!
	But, leaving these vain trifles of men's souls,
	Tell me what is that Lucifer thy lord?
MEPHIST:	Arch-regent and commander of all spirits.
FAUST:	Was not that Lucifer an angel once?
MEPHIST:	Yes, Faustus, and most dearly lov'd of God.
FAUST:	How comes it, then, that he is prince of devils?
MEPHIST:	O, by aspiring pride and insolence;
	For which God threw him from the face of heaven.
FAUST:	And what are you that live with Lucifer?
MEPHIST:	Unhappy spirits that fell with Lucifer,
	Conspir'd against our God with Lucifer,
	And are forever damn'd with Lucifer.
FAUST:	Where are you damn'd?

[1] indirectly
[2] Satan
[3] Paradise

107

MEPHIST: In hell.
FAUST: How comes it, then, that thou art out of hell?
MEPHIST: Why, this is hell, nor am I out of it.
            Think'st thou that I, who saw the face of God,
            And tasted the eternal joys of heaven,
            Am not tormented with ten thousand hells,
            In being depriv'd of everlasting bliss?
            O, Faustus, leave these frivolous demands,
            Which strike a terror to my fainting soul!
FAUST: What, is great Mephistophilis so passionate
            For being deprived of the joys of heaven?
            Learn thou of Faustus manly fortitude,
            And scorn those joys thou never shalt possess.

(a) Summarise the main points that arise from the discussion between
    Faustus and Mephistophilis.
(b) What impression do you gain of the character of the two speakers?
(c) Do you find this extract an effective piece of dramatic writing? Give
    full reasons for your opinion.

3. Read the extract carefully then answer the questions that follow.

    [*Semi-darkness*]

PIZARRO: This is probably our last night. If we die, what will we
            have gone for?
DE SOTO: Spain. Christ.
PIZARRO: I envy you, Cavalier.
DE SOTO: For what?
PIZARRO: Your service. God. King. It's all simple for you.
DE SOTO: No, sir, it's not simple. But it's what I've chosen.
PIZARRO: Yes. And what have I chosen?
DE SOTO: To be a King yourself. Or as good, if we win here.
PIZARRO: And what's that at my age? Not only swords turn into
            bars of metal. Sceptres too. What's left, De Soto?
DE SOTO: What you told me in Spain. A name for ballads. The
            man of Honour has three good lives: The Life Today.
            The Life to Come. The Life of Fame.
PIZARRO: Fame is long. Death is longer....Does anyone ever die
            for anything? I thought so once. Life was fierce with
            feeling. It was all hope, like on that boy. Swords shone
            and armour sang, and cheese bit you, and kissing

burned and Death—ah, death was going to make an exception in my case. I couldn't believe I was ever going to die. But once you know it—really know it—it's all over. You know you've been cheated, and nothing's the same again.

DE SOTO: Cheated?

PIZARRO: Time cheats us all the way. Children, yes—having children goes some steps to defeating it. Nothing else. It would have been good to have a son.

DE SOTO: Did you never think to marry?

PIZARRO: With my parentage? The only women who would have had me weren't the sort you married. Spain's a pile of horsedung.... When I began to think of a world here, something in me was longing for a new place like a country after rain, washed clear of all the badges and barriers, the pebbles men drop to tell them where they are on a plain that's got no landmarks. I used to look after women with hope, but they didn't have much time for me. One of them said—what was it?—my soul was frostbitten. That's a word for your—Frostbitten. How goes it man?

VASCA [off]: A clear night, sir. Everything clear.

PIZARRO: I had a girl once, on a rock by the Southern Ocean. I lay with her one afternoon in winter, wrapped up in her against the cold, and the sea-fowl screaming, and it was the best hour of my life. I felt then that sea-water and bird-droppings and the little pits in human flesh were all linked together for some great end right out of the net of words to catch. Not just my words, but anyone's. Then I lost it. Time came back. For always.

(a) Comment on the tone and atmosphere of this extract.
(b) Comment on the use of dialogue here.
(c) What insights do we gain from the extract into the character of Pizarro?

4. Read the extract carefully then answer the questions that follow.

[JACK WORTHING *is in the middle of proposing to* GWENDOLEN *when her mother,* LADY BRACKNELL, *enters.*]

LADY BRACKNELL: Mr Worthing! Rise, sir, from this semi-recum-

	bent posture. It is most indecorous.
GWENDOLEN:	Mama! [*He tries to rise; she restrains him.*] I must beg you to retire. This is no place for you. Besides, Mr Worthing has not quite finished yet.
LADY BRACKNELL:	Finished what, may I ask?
GWENDOLEN:	I am engaged to Mr Worthing, mamma. [*They rise together.*]
LADY BRACKNELL:	Pardon me, you are not engaged to anyone. When you do became engaged to someone, I, or your father, should his health permit him, will inform you of the fact. An engagement should come on a young girl as a surprise, pleasant or unpleasant, as the case may be. It is hardly a matter that she could be allowed to arrange for herself.... And now I have a few questions to put to you, Mr Worthing. While I am making these inquiries, you, Gwendolen, will wait for me below in the carriage.
GWENDOLEN:	[*reproachfully*]: Mamma!
LADY BRACKNELL:	In the carriage, Gwendolen! [*Gwendolen goes to the door. She and Jack blow kisses to each other behind Lady Bracknell's back. Lady Bracknell looks vaguely about as if she could not understand what the noise was. Finally turns round*] Gwendolen, the carriage!
GWENDOLEN:	Yes, Mamma. [*Goes out, looking back at Jack*]
LADY BRACKNELL [*sitting down*]:	You can take a seat, Mr Worthing. [*Looks in her pocket for note-book and pencil*]
JACK:	Thank you, Lady Bracknell, I prefer standing.
LADY BRACKNELL [*pencil and note-book in hand*]:	I feel bound to tell you that you are not down on my list of eligible young men, although I have the same list as the dear Duchess of Bolton has. We work together, in fact. However, I am quite ready to enter your name, should your answers be what a really affectionate mother requires. Do you smoke?
JACK:	Well, yes, I must admit I smoke.
LADY BRACKNELL:	I am glad to hear it. A man should always

	have an occupation of some kind. There are far too many idle men in London as it is. How old are you?
JACK:	Twenty-nine.
LADY BRACKNELL:	A very good age to be married at. I have always been of the opinion that a man who desires to get married should know either everything or nothing. Which do you know?
JACK: [*after some hesitation*]: I know nothing, Lady Bracknell.
LADY BRACKNELL:	I am pleased hear it. I do not approve of anything that tampers with natural ignorance. Ignorance is like a delicate exotic fruit; touch it and the bloom is gone. The whole theory of modern education is radically unsound. Fortunately in England, at any rate, education produces no effect whatsoever. If it did, it would prove a serious danger to the upper classes,and probably lead to acts of violence in Grosvenor Square. What is your income?
JACK:	Between seven and eight thousand a year.
LADY BRACKNELL [*makes a note in her book*]: In land, or in investments?
JACK:	In investments, chiefly.
LADY BRACKNELL:	That is satisfactory. What between the duties expected of one during one's lifetime, and the duties exacted from one after one's death, land has ceased to be either a profit or a pleasure. It gives one position, and prevents one from keeping it up. That's all that can be said about land.

(a) Comment on the use of language, character, tone, gesture, etc. to promote humour in this extract.
(b) Comment on the dramatic presentation of this scene.

5. Read the extract carefully then answer the questions that follow.

DUCHESS:	Now what you please, What death?
BOSOLA:	Strangling: here are your executioners.
DUCHESS:	I forgive them:

	The apoplexy, catarrh, or cough o'th' lungs
	Would do as much as they do.
BOSOLA:	Doth not death fright you?
DUCHESS:	Who would be afraid on't?
	Knowing to meet such excellent company
	In th' other world.
BOSOLA:	Yet, methinks,
	The manner of your death should much afflict you,
	This cord should terrify you?
DUCHESS:	Not a whit:
	What would it pleasure me, to have my throat cut
	With diamonds? or to be smothered
	With cassia? or to be shot to death, with pearls?
	I know death hath ten thousand several doors
	For men to take their "Exits": and 'tis found
	They go on such strange geometrical hinges,
	You may open them both ways: any way, for Heaven's sake,
	So I were out of your whispering. Tell my brothers
	That I perceive death, now I am well awake,
	Best gift is, they can give, or I can take.
	I would fain put off my last woman's fault,
	I'll'd not be tedious to you.
EXECUTIONERS:	We are ready.
DUCHESS:	Dispose my breath how please you, but my body
	Bestow upon my women, will you?
EXECUTIONERS:	Yes.
DUCHESS:	Pull, and pull strongly, for your able strength
	Must pull down heaven upon me:
	Yet stay, heaven gates are not so highly arch'd
	As princes' palaces: they that enter there
	Must go upon their knees. Come violent death,
	Serve for mandragora to make me sleep;
	Go tell my brothers,when I am laid out,
	Then then may feed in quiet.
	[*They strangle her.*]

(a) What insights into the Duchess's character are offered in this scene?

(b) Comment on the use of language in this extract?

(c) This scene is taken from a typical Revenge Play. What do you

112

understand by this term and what elements of this scene are characteristic of this type of Drama?

SECTION B

1. Read carefully this extract from *Henry V*, then answer the questions that follow.

KING HENRY: Once more unto the breach, dear friends, once more;
Or close the wall up with our English dead!
In peace there's nothing so becomes a man
As modest stillness and humility:
But when the blast of war blows in our ears,
Then imitate the action of the tiger;
Stiffen the sinews, summon up the blood,
Disguise fair nature with hard-favour'd rage;
Then lend the eye a terrible aspect;
Let it pry through the portage of the head
Like the brass cannon; let the brow o'erwhelm it
As fearfully as doth a galled rock
O'erhang and jutty his confounded base,
Swill'd with the wild and wasteful ocean.
Now set the teeth and stretch the nostril wide;
Hold hard the breath, and bend up every spirit
To his full height!—On, on, you noble English,
Whose blood is fet from fathers of war-proof!—
Fathers that, like so many Alexanders,
Have in these parts from morn till even fought,
And sheath'd their swords for lack of argument:—
Dishonour not your mothers; now attest
That those whom you call'd fathers did beget you!
Be copy now to men of grosser blood,
And teach them how to war!—And you, good yeomen,
Whose limbs were made in England, show us here
The mettle of your pasture; let us swear
That you are worth your breeding: which I doubt not;
For there is none of you so mean and base,
That hath not noble lustre in your eyes.

I see you stand like greyhounds in the slips,
Straining upon the start. The game's afoot:
Follow your spirit; and upon this charge
Cry—God for Harry! England!—and Saint George!

(a) Summarise the different types of appeal and exhortation Henry
employs here to inspire his men in battle.
(b) Comment on the tone and atmosphere of this speech.
(c) Comment on the use of language in this extract.

2. Read this extract from *As You Like It*, then answer the questions that
follow.

JAQUES: I thank you for your company; but, good faith, I had as
lief have been myself alone.
ORLANDO: And so had I; but yet, for fashion's sake, I thank you
too for your society.
JAQUES: God be with you: let's meet as little as we can.
ORLANDO: I do desire we may be better strangers.
JAQUES: I pray you, mar no more trees with writing love-songs
in their barks.
ORLANDO: I pray you, mar no more of my verses with reading
them ill-favouredly.
JAQUES: Rosalind is your love's name?
ORLANDO: Yes, just.
JAQUES: I do not like her name.
ORLANDO: There was no thought of pleasing you when she was
christened.
JAQUES: What stature is she of?
ORLANDO: Just as high as my heart.
JAQUES: You are full of pretty answers. Have you not bee ac-
quainted with goldsmiths' wives, and conned them
out of rings?
ORLANDO: Not so; but I answer you right painted cloth, from
whence you have studied your questions.
JAQUES: You have a nimble wit: I think it was made of Ata-
lanta's heels. Will you sit down with me? and we two
will rail against our mistress the world, and all our
misery.
ORLANDO: I will chide no breather in the world but myself, against
whom I know most faults.
JAQUES: The worst fault you have is to be in love.

ORLANDO: 'Tis a fault I will not change for your best virtue. I am weary of you.

JAQUES: By my troth, I was seeking for a fool when I found you.

ORLANDO: He is drowned in the brook; look but in, and you shall see him.

JAQUES: There I shall see mine own figure.

ORLANDO: Which I take to be either a fool or a cipher.[1]

JAQUES: I'll tarry no longer with you: farewell good Signior Love.

ORLANDO: I am glad of your departure: adieu, good Monsieur Melancholy.

(a) Analyse the style and tone of this exchange.
(b) Comment on the use of wit and language in this extract.
(c) What is your impression of the two speakers?

3. Read carefully the extract from *Hamlet*, then answer the questions that follow.

[*Enter Ghost*]

HAMLET: Angels and ministers of grace defend us!—
Be thou a spirit of health or goblin damn'd,
Bring with thee airs from heaven or blasts from hell,
Be thy intents wicked or charitable,
Thou com'st in such a questionable shape
That I will speak to thee: I'll call thee Hamlet,
King, father, royal Dane: O, answer me!
Let me not burst in ignorance; but tell
Why they canoniz'd bones, hearsed in death,
Have burst their cerements; why thy sepulchre,
Wherein we saw thee quietly in-urn'd,
Hath op'd his ponderous and marble jaws
To cast thee up again! What may this mean,
That thou, dead corse, again in complete steel,
Revisit'st thus the glimpses of the moon,
Making night hideous, and we fools of nature
So horridly to shake our disposition
With thoughts beyond the reaches of our souls?
Say, why is this? wherefore? what should we do?

[1]person of no importance

HORATIO:	It beckons you to go away with it,
	As if it some impartment did desire
	To you alone.
MARCELLUS:	Look with what courteous action
	It waves you to a more removed ground;
	But do not go with it.
HORATIO:	No, by no means.
HAMLET:	It will not speak; then I will follow it.
HORATIO:	Do not, my lord.
HAMLET:	Why, what should be the fear?
	I do not set my life at a pin's fee;
	And for my soul, what can it do to that,
	Being a thing immortal as itself?
	It waves me forth again;—I'll follow it.
HORATIO:	What if it tempt you toward the flood, my lord.
	Or the dreadful summit of the cliff
	That beetles o'er his base into the sea,
	And there assume some other terrible form,
	Which might deprive your sovreignty of reason,
	And draw you into madness? think of it;
	The very place puts toys of desperation,
	Without more motive, into every brain
	That looks so many fathoms to the sea
	And hears it roar beneath.
HAMLET:	It waves me still.—
	Go on; I'll follow thee.
MARCELLUS:	You shall not go, my lord.
HAMLET:	Hold off your hands.
HORATIO:	Be rul'd; you shall not go.
HAMLET:	My fate cries out,
	And makes each petty artery in this body
	As hardy as the Nemean lion's nerve.—
	[*Ghost beckons*]
	Still I am call'd;—unhand me, gentlemen;—
	[*Breaking from them*]
	By heaven, I'll make a ghost of him that lets me.
	I say, away!—Go on; I'll follow thee.

(a) What is the dilemma confronting Hamlet in this extract?
(b) How is Hamlet's state of mind conveyed in this scene?
(c) Examine the use of imagery to create dramatic atmosphere here.

4. Read carefully the extract from *Coriolanus*, then answer the questions that follow.

[*Enter a company of mutinous citizens, with staves, clubs, and other weapons*]

1 CIT:	Before we proceed further, hear me speak.
CITIZENS:	Speak, speak.
1 CIT:	You are all resolved rather to die than to famish?
CITIZENS:	Resolved, resolved.
1 CIT:	First, you know Caius Marcius is chief enemy to the people.
CITIZENS:	We know't, we know't.
1 CIT:	Let us kill him, and we'll have corn at our own price. Is't a verdict?
CITIZENS:	No more talking on't; let it be done: away, away!
2 CIT:	One word, good citizens.
1 CIT:	We are accounted poor citizens; the patricians good. What authority surfeits on would relieve us: if they would yield us but the superfluity, while it were wholesome, we might guess they relieved us humanely; but they think we are too dear: the leanness hat afflicts us, the object of our misery, is an inventory to particularise their abundance; our sufferance is gain to them.—Let us revenge this with our pikes ere we become rakes: for the gods know I speak this in hunger for bread, not in thirst for revenge.
2 CIT:	Would you proceed especially against Caius Marcius?
1 CIT:	Against him first: he's a very dog to the commonalty.
2 CIT:	Consider you what services he has done for his country?
1 CIT:	Very well; and could be content to give him good report for't, but that he pays himself with being proud.
2 CIT:	Nay but speak not maliciously.
1 CIT:	I say unto you, what he hath done famously he did it to that end: though soft-conscienced men can be content to say it was for his country, he did it to please his mother, and to be partly proud; which he is, even to the altitude of his virtue.

(a) This extract is the opening of the play. What is there in this scene to promote audience interest in what will follow?

(b) In what ways does Shakespeare lend an individual character to Citizen 1 and Citizen 2?

5. Read the extract from *Antony and Cleopatra* carefully, then answer the questions that follow.

[*Enobarbus is describing the first meeting of Antony and Cleopatra.*]

ENOBARBUS: The barge she sat in, like a burnish'd throne,
Burn'd on the water: the poop was beaten gold;
Purple the sails, and so perfumed that
The winds were love-sick with them; the oars were silver,
Which to the tune of flutes kept stroke, and made
The water which they beat to follow faster,
As amorous of their strokes. For her own person,
It begar'd all description: she did lie
In her pavilion,—cloth-of-gold, of tissue,—
O'er-picturing that Venus where we see
The fancy out-work nature: on each side her
Stood pretty dimpled boys, like smiling Cupids,
With divers-colour'd fans, whose wind did seem
To glow the delicate cheeks which they did cool,
And what they undid did.
AGRIPPA: O, rare for Antony!
ENOBARBUS: Her gentlewomen, like the Nereids,
So many mermaids, tended her i' the eyes,
And made their bends adornings: at the helm
A seeming mermaid steers: the silken tackle
Swell the touches of those flower-soft hands
That yarely frame the office. From the barge
A strange invisible perfume hits the sense
Of the adjacent wharfs. The city cast
Her people out upon her; and Antony,
Enthron'd i' the market-place, did sit alone,
Whistling to the air; which, but for vacancy,
Had gone to gaze on Cleopatra too,
And made a gap in nature.
AGRIPPA: Rare Egyptian!
ENOBARBUS: Upon her landing, Antony sent to her,
Invited her to supper: she replied
It should be better he became her guest;

Which she entreated: our courteous Antony
Whom ne'er the word of "No" woman heard speak,
Being barber'd ten times o'er, goes to the feast,
And, for his ordinary[1], pays his heart
For what his eyes eat only.

(a) What subtle impressions of the characters of Antony and Cleopatra and of their relationship are conveyed in this account?
(b) Comment on the use of imagery in this extract.

6. Select 4 passages from each of the plays by Shakespeare that you are studying that seem to you to be particularly significant to the play as a whole. Consider each passage in terms of:

(a) its dramatic significance within the play;
(b) what important aspects of characterisation the passage reveals;
(c) what dramatic elements are employed by the passage to achieve its significant effect;
(d) the use of language in the extract.

SECTION C

This section offers generalised essay topics that may be applied to any play the student may be studying in depth.

1. Analyse the *dramatic significance* of the depth played by three *minor* characters in any play you are currently studying.
2. Analyse, in detail, the precise means by which we are given insights into the character of one of the protagonists in a play you are currently studying.
3. Consider a play you are currently studying. Prepare a graph, indicating the "peaks" of the more dramatic, or significant action in the play. (On a scale of, say, 1 to 5, 1 would represent the "quiet" scenes, 5 the most "dramatic".) From this information, write an essay on the structure, pace and rhythm of the play's plot.
4. What do you understand by the terms "realism" and "psychological realism"? How would you relate these concepts to a play you are currently studying?

[1]public meal

5. What do you consider to be the central theme or issue behind one of the plays you are studying? How does the dramatist develop this theme? What do you feel is the dramatist's own position in relation to this theme?

6. Analyse the ways in which language is used to create a particular tone, mood and atmosphere in a play you are currently studying.

7. Consider the potential of any play you are studying for providing an audience with dramatic spectacle.

8. Consider one of the plays you are currently studying. In what ways does the play represent the typical issues and concerns of its own time? What issues and concerns within the play are relevant to future audiences?

9. Write a personal review of your *own* impressions of one of the plays you are currently studying.

10. Consider one of the plays you are currently studying in terms of the main elements of Drama—plot, character, theme and language. What do you consider to be the play's strengths and weaknesses in these areas?

CHAPTER 14

GLOSSARY OF USEFUL TERMS

Absurd	See Chapter 3: "The Forms of Drama".
Aside	Words spoken by an actor that are not meant to be heard by the other persons on the stage.
Caricature	One-dimensional, undeveloped dramatic portrait.
Catastrophe	Climax of the main action in a play, usually suggesting fatal or tragic consequences.
Catharsis	"Purification" or "purging". Aristotle's concept that our thoughts and emotions are relieved and "purified" by the experience of watching great Drama.
Charade	Form of mime, riddle or pretense.
Characterisation	The means by which a dramatist develops the audience's insight and perception of the character of his dramatic personae.
Climax	Culmination or peak of the dramatic action.
Comedic	Adjective from "comedy".
Comedy	See Chapter 3: "The Forms of Drama".
Confidant	Dramatic character, usually minor, in whom the main characters confide their deepest thoughts, feelings or intentions.
Crisis	Moment at which the play's central conflict must be resolved one way or the other.
Dialogue	Words spoken between characters in a play.
Dramatic	Relating to Drama as a whole, or a play in particu-

lar, as in the *dramatic significance* of a certain scene. Care should be taken to distinguish between this technical usage of the word and its more modern shading of "striking" or "vivid".

Elevated	Expression, character or passage that is "heightened" and more formal than usual.
Exposition	Means by which crucial information about situation, plot and character are imparted to the audience.
Farce	See Chapter 3: "The Forms of Drama".
Fatal Flaw	Aristotle's concept of the basic human weakness (ambition, pride, jealousy, etc.) that destroys an otherwise noble nature.
Heroic	Used to describe a style of language, character, or action that is grand and "high-flown".
Historical Drama	See Chapter 3: "The Forms of Drama".
Hubris	Excessive pride that usually leads to tragedy.
Knockabout	Unsophisticated, visual humour usually found in Farce. Also known as "slapstick".
Masque	See Chapter 3: "The Forms of Drama".
Melodrama	See Chapter 3: "The Forms of Drama".
Mime	Forms of communication without words, through elaborate gesture and movement. Also known as "Dumb-show".
Naturalism	Applied to plays in which the dramatist attempts a totally faithful, "true to life" presentation. See *Realism*.
Persona	Character in a play. Note the plural, *personae*.
Plot	See Chapter 4: "Plot".
Production	All the combined physical components (costume, lighting, set, make-up, etc.) that constitute the play in performance. The elements of production will reflect the director's interpretation of the play.
Protagonist	The leading character, or characters, in a play. Sometimes known as the "hero" or "heroine". Protagonist is a more precise term, as "hero" has modern associations that may not be relevant.
Realism	See Chapter 2: "The Essence of Drama".
Resolution	The moment at the end of the play (usually) when the major issues, conflicts, etc. are "resolved", or "sorted out", and the final perspective emerges.
Satire	See Chapter 3: "The Forms of Drama".
Sensationalism	Use of extreme, violent and unsubtle demands upon

	an audience's emotions.
Soliloquy	Words spoken by a character, alone on the stage, for the benefit of the audience alone. An attempt to offer the character's innermost thoughts and feelings, a sort of "thinking out loud".
Stereotype	Clichéd, one-dimensional character (i.e. "the jealous husband", etc.) who is not developed in any "rounded" way.
Stock	Adjective applied to describe a type of character or situation (or even language) that has been used many times before in the same "formula fashion". See also *Caricature, Stereotype.*
Suspension of Disbelief	What Coleridge saw as the audience's necessary "pretense" of accepting what they see on the stage as "real life", without which the whole process of Drama becomes meaningless.
The Three Unities	See Chapter 4: "Plot".
Tragedy	See Chapter 3: "The Forms of Drama".
Tragi-comedy	Play that blends the elements of both Tragedy and Comedy in equal measure.
Verse Drama	See Chapter 3: "The Forms of Drama".